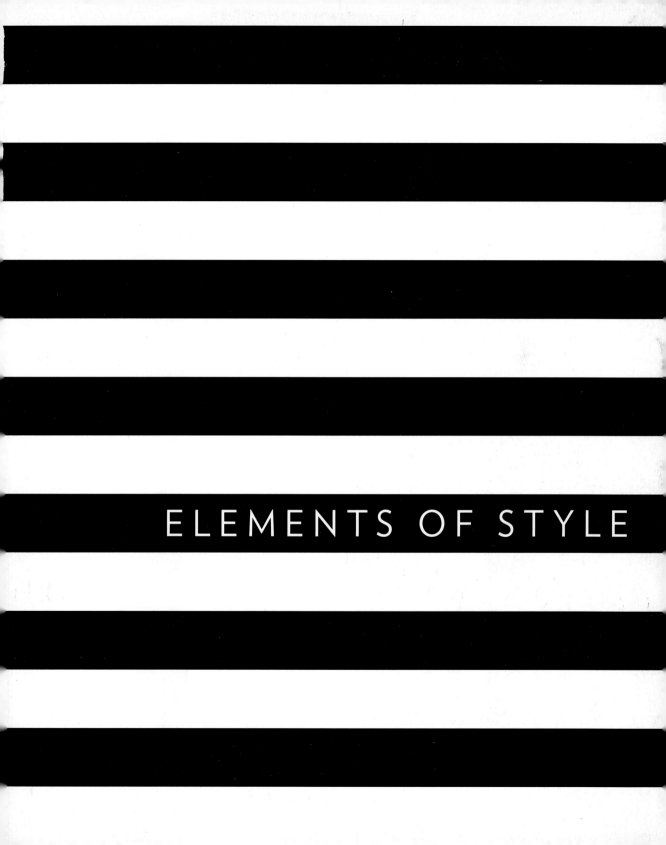

ELEMENTS OF STYLE

ELEMENTS OF STYLE

DESIGNING A HOME & A LIFE

ERIN GATES

SIMON & SCHUSTER

New York London Toronto Sydney New Delhi

SIMON & SCHUSTER
1230 Avenue of the Americas
New York, NY 10020

First Simon & Schuster hardcover edition October 2014

SIMON & SCHUSTER and colophon are registered trademarks of
Simon & Schuster, Inc.

For information about special discounts for bulk purchases, please
contact Simon & Schuster Special Sales at 1-866-506-1949 or
business@simonandschuster.com.

The Simon & Schuster Speakers Bureau can bring authors to your live event.
For more information or to book an event, contact the
Simon & Schuster Speakers Bureau at 1-866-248-3049 or visit our website at
www.simonspeakers.com.

Photography by MICHAEL J. LEE, MICHAEL PARTENIO, SARAH
WINCHESTER, ERIC ROTH, and DANIELLE MOSS
Illustrations by ANNE HARWELL McELHANEY
Interior design by JENNIFER K. BEAL DAVIS
Jacket design by JENNIFER K. BEAL DAVIS

Manufactured in China

1 3 5 7 9 10 8 6 4 2

Library of Congress Cataloging-in-Publication Data
Gates, Erin T.
Elements of style : designing a home and a life / Erin T. Gates.
p. cm
1. Interior decoration. I. Title.
NK2115.G325 2014
747—dc23   2014012101

ISBN 978-1-4767-4487-2
ISBN 978-1-4767-4488-9 (ebook)

To Mom and Dad, who taught me how to build and fill a home with love;
Andrew, who is my home wherever he is (and however he's decorated);
and, most gratefully, my blog readers, who made this all happen

CONTENTS

FOREWORD

Take a deep breath and jump in." That was the title of Erin's first blog post on April 3, 2007. As it turns out, it was a very deep breath and an Olympic-level jump, especially for someone who is not an entrepreneur at heart. She has done what so many of us want to do—create a career by following a passion. But that first step to following your passion is scary.

If you have read Erin's blog, *Elements of Style,* you already know a lot about her. She is funny, opinionated, stylish, honest, open, sympathetic, and caring. She puts it all out there for everyone to see. She is brave and bold. She has an effect on people she comes into contact with. That has certainly been true for me.

OPPOSITE: Modern art juxtaposed against traditional interior architecture makes for an interesting and unexpected mix.

ERIN LIKES ME.

As corny as that sounds, it is an important distinction. I hope it goes without saying that she loves me. But at times in marriage, it is easier to love than to like. We are very different people. And even though the saying "opposites attract" is true, it doesn't mean such relationships always work out. I am not an easy person to be married to (easy to love, easy to live with, but not married to). That is actually one quality we share. She says she sees something special in me, but the truth is, I am reflecting her. One of my favorite movie quotes was said by Jack Nicholson in *As Good As It Gets*—"You make me want to be a better man." Erin *makes* me a better man.

ERIN MAKES SURE WE TAKE THE SCENIC ROUTE IN LIFE.

She puts so much effort into our lives. At times I take it for granted, especially the small details like a lit candle (they're everywhere) or the interior color of a cabinet no one sees but us. She takes great care with these details that are seemingly insignificant but when put together, create a home. I have given up arguing that it is unnecessary to paint that little space no one will ever see or change the knob on the cabinet in the mudroom. Those

things, I have come to realize, are the difference between a house and a home. They are the difference between the direct route and the scenic route.

ERIN INSPIRES ME.

Every so often I am asked if her success intimidates me, if it makes me feel like less of a man. I would be lying if I said the thought never crossed my mind. But it doesn't linger. What replaces it is motivation. I wake up every morning trying to find the kind of energy, focus, and passion Erin has. Every night, when the day is finally done, we sit with a glass of wine on our couch, with our dogs, to relax. Except it isn't quite done for her. She begins to research and write tomorrow's blog post. When this first began, I was concerned she was working too hard. But what I have realized is that she is so busy during the day with this book or a photo shoot or a client or an ever-growing list of things she adds to her repertoire, that the blog is her way to relax. It's enjoyable for her. While it's not always effortless, not always stress free, she would be doing this whether she had ten blog readers or ten million. Whether she had a thousand things to do the next day or none. She is constantly reminding me of just how much is possible. She is doing what she was meant to do. And despite having a very healthy dose

of self-doubt, she is the most confident person I know. Not because she has life figured out, but because she doesn't and she puts it out there anyway. She is maddeningly true to herself. It may be the quality I admire most.

I don't know why she asked me to write the foreword to her book. There are far more famous, influential, and worthy writers, designers, and fashionistas who should be writing it. Even so, it has been worth the effort to try and put into words exactly what she means to me. I admit that, until now, I have not taken the time to put my feelings into words. I guess I have believed that it goes without saying. But it shouldn't. I am proud of her for so many things. Being able to write this book is just one in a long line. I hope it inspires you in many ways. But if you take one thing from the following pages, I hope it is that home is what you make it. It is about being with the ones you love and having a space that allows you to leave the outside world behind and focus on the truly important things. Those around you.

ANDREW GATES
DECEMBER 2013

INTRODUCTION

In the time I have been designing homes for a living, I have lived in five. Some I owned, some I rented, some I loved, and some I wanted to demolish gleefully with a wrecking ball. Some were large, others were small, some needed work while others I wasn't allowed to work on. Each place I've called home has had its own look, furniture arrangement, and color scheme, but what all these spaces had in common was their role in sheltering me and my life story. When I think of each apartment or condo, I recall specific memories—happy and sad—that make up who I am and the life I've led. While a home provides shelter and a place to gather, it is also the safe place where

OPPOSITE: A bold, fun entryway welcomes you home.

we can express our feelings and enjoy some of the most important and meaningful events in our lives.

Therefore, designing a home is a very personal venture. I strongly believe that a home provides a canvas on which we can illustrate who we are; your space should look like you and no one else (even if you are using an interior designer). While some designers love a blank slate and the freedom to do whatever they want, I prefer to work with clients who have an opinion, a story, and unique artifacts collected over time: a dresser found in an antique market in the country, a desk from an adored father, art bought on a magical trip across France. I always want the end result to be the best possible version of their taste, filtered through my knowledge of design concepts and sources. While helping them create homes they love, I have learned so much from them as well. I've reflected on my own life through my work, figuring out what I personally love and who I want to be.

It's this practice of introspection that led me to share not only pretty spaces and design tips on my blog, *Elements of*

Style, but tales from my life too—triumphs, failures, funny moments and poignant ones. I love the way spaces tell stories and how stories are born from creating spaces, and from that love this book was born. Organized by rooms in the home, this book contains inspirational images of interiors and honest design advice as well as personal anecdotes that relate to each space—from the fear I felt relocating to the suburbs from the city, to the realities of renovating a kitchen (not all fun and games, as it turns out, even for a designer!).

There has been nothing more gratifying to me than to hear from others that I've helped them in some way, from finding the perfect crib for their expected little one to sharing a painful memory that allowed them to feel not so alone in this world. I hope this book helps and encourages you on your journey to creating a home and life you love.

ERIN GATES

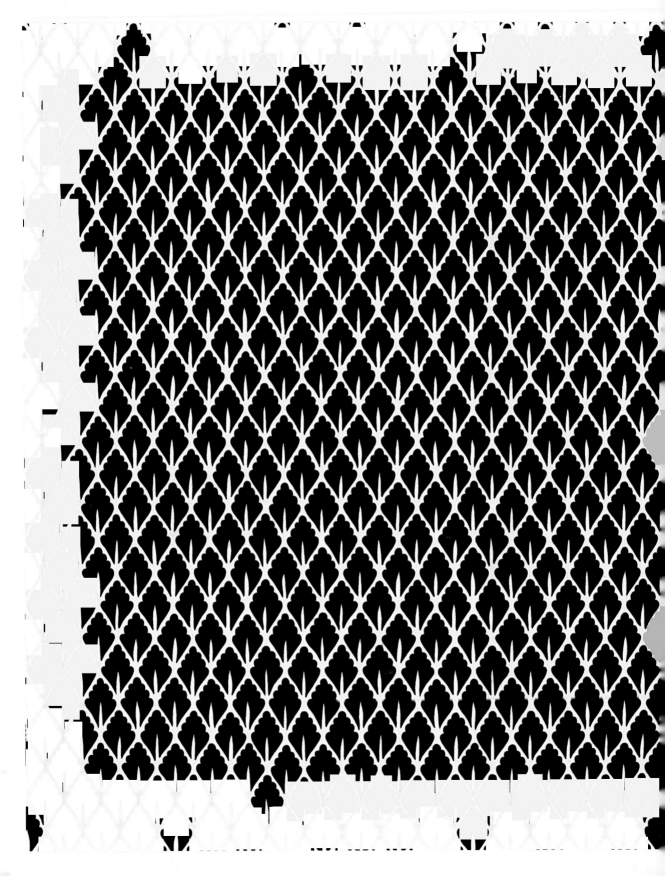

THE ENTRY

WELCOME TO SUBURBIA – WHEN CAN I GO HOME?

I was living the chic thirtysomething's dream, happily residing in a ridiculously overpriced rental apartment on one of Boston's nicest streets. Charm surrounded me on all sides in the form of brick row houses, tree-lined sidewalks, little cafés and boutiques . . . oh, and noisy, annoying neighbors. Ahh, there it is. The one element of city living that might be enough to push the otherwise city-or-die type to the brink. Or to the 'burbs. My husband, Andrew, and I had suffered many an annoying neighbor, from the piano player who practiced from 10 to 11 p.m., to the family with kids who ran around upstairs like it was a friggin' playground, to our most recent neighbor, she of the 2 a.m. heel-clomping escapades. I started forming theories

OPPOSITE: Our entryway extends into our living room, as it does in most small spaces. This console serves as a place for us to drop our keys and mail, as well as a place for decorative accessories. Underneath, we tuck additional seating for entertaining in the form of a pair of garden stools.

3

about this nocturnal creature, such as: she must be a nurse working odd hours. Or a stripper. Or maybe she sleepwalked into her closet nightly and put on her Manolos and then practiced her Zumba moves. Whatever the case, it was enough to make me chuck my heels at the ceiling.

So, given the noise and an economy in which mortgage rates hit an all-time low, we decided we should buy a place of our own again. Andrew wanted a real house, with our own four walls and roof, while my first proclamation was that it had to still be in the city. And within a five block radius of our current apartment. And if you live in Boston (or any big city) you know what that means: a cool three-quarters of a million bucks for maybe two bedrooms, at the top of four flights of stairs, with no air-conditioning or parking and uncertain "noise issues." After attending some seriously discouraging open houses, I suggested perhaps we keep renting for one more year while we continued to look for the perfect condo. But after Andrew showed me his calculations of just how much money we'd be burning through, I decided that maybe I should listen to his idea of looking just outside the city at something a bit more detached. After all, he said, we did need to "think about our future," which translated into "let's get you knocked up, babycakes." Because, as we

all know, no hip, stylish couple would ever move to the suburbs if children were not in the picture.

Cue panic. I never craved the stereotypical American dream. My vision of the whole white picket fence with 2.5 kids and a station wagon was instead a town house in the city with 2.5 dogs and a parking spot. I'm not saying I never contemplated kids, I just had yet to feel that burning desire for them, which I have always assumed would feel like a pile of hot coals burning in your uterus, an undeniable yearning. And when you've been married for eight years and are in your early thirties, this lack of offspring can cause a lot of confusion and trauma. Particularly in my mother. But banking on that baby fever kicking in at some point in the next decade, I did have to consider the possibility of needing more room than we could afford in downtown Boston. So I gave in and said I'd look, just look, at some houses in the very nearby suburbs.

The more we looked, however, the more I was convinced (and secretly relieved) we wouldn't find anything there. Many of the homes in our price range needed major updates. Considering I design homes for a living, we had no children, and my father happens to own an architecture firm, we were the most perfect people to tackle a renovation project. I knew what was possible for many of the houses we viewed—not just with paint and lighting, but with brawn, two-by-fours, and a backhoe. But nothing was clicking.

See, I don't just design homes, I have emotional affairs with houses. I grew up taking Sunday drives with my dad and my siblings to various towns in New England while he explained to us kids the beauty of a specific trim, roofline, and windows. I soon learned to drool over dormers and pant heavily for a good portico. So I needed to feel something more.

Case in point: our increasingly exasperated agent insisted we see a house in the best location in town. And she was right about the location—two blocks from restaurants and shops (and Starbucks! Praise be!) and a mere twelve-minute drive into the city. But as we pulled up, my gut reaction was *oh hellllllll no* (while mentally snapping my fingers in a Z formation). Ugly green shutters, an interior covered in metallic wallpaper (the bad kind), and soaked in smoke. The kicker? It was $50,000 over our budget. Yet despite the location and the fact that I knew I could tear out the wallpaper and air out the smoke, I simply could not get on board. I felt no emotional connection to this house, which is to me the most important element in making a house a

MY VERSION OF THE WHOLE WHITE PICKET FENCE WITH 2.5 KIDS AND A STATION WAGON WAS INSTEAD A TOWN HOUSE IN THE CITY WITH 2.5 DOGS AND A PARKING SPOT.

home. This house was the "nice guy" you know would be so good for you to date but you find him dull and kind of like your brother. I wanted to say to it, "Sorry, house; it isn't you, it's me. Can we still be friends?" As I dithered, in my typical fashion, some other couple jumped on the chance to buy Nice Guy House and off they rode into the sunset.

Instead of the Nice Guy, I needed the lover—I mean, house—that would wine and dine me into suburban submission. And, lo and behold, I found it. The house was, of course, out of our price range, but not so much so that perhaps we couldn't haggle. As our car rolled up to the address, I nearly jumped out of the car and did the ol' tuck and roll just to get closer to it. My dream house! A *Father of the Bride* house, if you will. Despite its odd additions and, yes, the price, I wanted this one something fierce. I knew it was supposed to be mine. So we made an offer and after some back-and-forth, got the house. I was elated beyond words (and already pulling out wallpaper samples).

I thought I knew enough not to be deceived by the guy whose smoking-hot exterior hides many relationship-ending flaws, but I had fallen in love before the home inspection. As the kind inspector circled the property and made notes, I noticed he looked a bit, well, concerned. As he approached us to reveal his findings, I could have sworn I heard the *Jaws* theme song playing. The house had everything wrong with it you could possibly imagine: mold, termites, water damage, bad electrical, old water main, structural issues, and a giant tree that threatened to crush it to smithereens should a hurricane approach. It was a modern day *Money Pit*. Just like that, we were back to square one.

But then the universe, as I have learned it often does, came through for me. The contract on Nice Guy House had fallen through. I began to look at it with new eyes, even though they were the eyes of a desperate woman who needed a place to call home. I pictured it with fresh paint, dark floors, and a new kitchen. I walked around the neighborhood and realized it was an insane location for the price. And it was built really well and in no threat of infestation or flooding. The seller was getting nervous, so we threw in a lowball offer and we got it. Let the celebration commence, right?

Wrong, because you know what happened next? I freaked. Like, ugly-crying-with-snot-running-out-my-nose freaked. When it wasn't mine, I wanted it. Now that it was, I wanted to light it on fire. (Pretty sure I also treated many

a boyfriend that way too.) Such is the struggle of being a raging perfectionist with a serious grass-is-greener complex. I was terrified to leave the city, and I knew I would get sweaty and panicky when there wasn't a Starbucks within a three-block radius. Plus we were still a childless couple who had no need for three bedrooms. I struggled not only with the idea of getting pregnant, but of accomplishing the feat.

But the money scared me more than anything. As a designer, of course I knew the cost of the necessary renovations and understood in theory that this perfectionist would have to be patient with the overhaul of my new home. (Another thing I am no good at. I tend to be the girl who starts tapping her foot and sending the waiter eye daggers when her wine order isn't taken five seconds after sitting down at dinner.)

The first night we spent in the house, everything was covered in construction dust and only half the rooms were painted. As I sat in my living room nursing a glass of pinot grigio and staring at a blotchy wall, I felt tears well up again as I contemplated the life choices I had made. I could be in the city right now meeting a friend for drinks and moseying home with not a care in the world. Instead, I'm sitting in this half torn-down house in suburbia, crying.

I looked at my husband happily scraping away at old flaky window mullions and my puppies chasing each other deliriously around their new yard and it hit me.

IT ISN'T JUST ABOUT ME ANYMORE.

It's about us. My family—its current members and those still to come. It's about investing in something that will shape and contain our stories from here on out. It's about spending money smartly and for the long-term. Not focusing solely on what makes me happy in the here and now, but what will make us happy moving forward, and as we grow as a family. These tobacco-stained walls and scuffed floors can be made beautiful again. That kitchen will someday be one of my own design—exactly as I've always wanted one to look. These changes are all helping me become the woman I've always hoped I would be.

When I said to Nice Guy House—now my house! On which I have a mortgage!—"It isn't you, it's me," that was actually true. It was me. My fear of the future, of leaving behind my old life of thirty-two restaurants within a five-minute walk—even of starting a family. Of the unknown pain, pleasure, and inevitable pitfalls that all come with growing up. Staying in one place by yourself is much easier than

changing, growing, and letting more love into your life. But together we will build memories here just as the family before us did.

The grieving owner let a few tears fall when handing over the keys to the house she had grown up and lived in her whole life. She wished us as happy a life in this house as she and her family had had. At the time I was too self-absorbed to wrap my brain around how lovely a sentiment that was. But as I sat there in the middle of move-in mess, seeing the happiness of those I loved more than anything, I finally got it. This is what it's all about.

Now I come home to a quiet house with a roaring fireplace and a sense of peace that can be hard to find in the constant social stimulation of the city. And there is fulfillment in working on a place I know I'll be in for many years. I am shocked to find that painting concrete floors fills me with a sense of accomplishment. I've tried to pinpoint just where this newfound sense of well-being came from, and I think I may have figured it out: I feel at ease and secure. I feel welcome. The Nice Guy turned out to be Mr. Right. And, don't worry: as you will see in the following pages, he did get one heck of a makeover.

CREATING A FUNCTIONAL & STYLISH ENTRY

The entry of a home serves a far larger purpose than just a place to hang a coat and toss a stack of mail. It introduces visitors to your house and tells a little bit about what they will find inside. A lot of people overlook this area when it's really one of the most important spaces to design well. Like a kitchen, it has to function efficiently—giving you a place to put coats, keys, mail, shoes, school stuff, sports equipment, and dog leashes. But it also has to be beautiful and give a first impression of your taste. That's a lot to accomplish in a relatively small space, but it can be done! Fear not, grasshoppers!

Entry sizes and types vary from the minuscule and multipurposed (like mine) to the large and grand, with double staircases and walk-in closets. But each one serves the same purpose, just on a different scale. When we first moved in, I had grand plans to have a mirror, a cute Lucite table, and a lantern in my entry. But after living there awhile, which you should always do before making design decisions, I realized it was too small for my plans. With the coat closet in the back of the house, we had to use one wall for hooks to hold my bevy of handbags as well as coats and a small storage basket for dog stuff. The way the door opened also made it impossible to install a hanging fixture, so I had to find a stylish flush-mount (it's possible, they DO actually exist). We have a console in our living room right off the entry that serves as

OPPOSITE: While our stairway is narrow and low, that did not stop me from making it a focal point by installing a gallery wall of favorite photos and prints. Hung haphazardly in mismatched frames this massive grouping actually creates a feeling of MORE space instead of less by keeping the eye busy and distracted from the space's shortcomings! The walls are painted in Benjamin Moore Balboa Mist.

before

a not-quite-perfect place for keys and mail, but I make it work with cute boxes for organization. I picked a custom leopard runner to dress up the stairs and opened the wall to one side to allow for a more open feeling (and to provide a glimpse of my gorgeous new kitchen!).

It's all about respecting how you live and not trying to create a space for some person who lives in a magazine. If it isn't designed to function for you, it won't ever feel right or look its best because it will be messy and awkward. You have to be honest with yourself about what you NEED versus what you WANT and also what you can AFFORD. Once you consider those three key things, you can then get down to making your entry absolute perfection.

ABOVE: During our renovations we opened up the small doorway from the entry into the dining room/kitchen, making it extra wide and bringing a more welcoming, open flow to the cramped space.

OPPOSITE: Our entryway is minuscule, so I decided to make one grand statement by carpeting the stairs in a luxurious and bold wool runner in my signature animal print! No apologies here for our lack of space. Embrace what you have and work with it; don't try to make it something it's not.

ABOVE: Details make all the difference. In order to make this utilitarian space special, I searched for and found a magnificently cool vintage brass coatrack to mount beside the front door. Since our ceiling is quite low and the door swing prevents anything lower, we used the most stylish flush-mount fixture we could find and left the drama to the stairs!

OPPOSITE: One thing we lack is a hall closet, having removed it in order to open up the hallway behind the stairs into the living room. So for now we get by with a coatrack by the front door and a separate set of coat hooks in a small mudroom at the back of the house. Ideal? No, but it works for us.

DEFINE YOUR STYLE: ENTRY

modern

Burled wood, hints of bling, and some graphic touches.

eclectic

Nailhead details, vintage rugs, and mixed-media gallery walls.

glamorous

Ladylike lighting, mirrored furniture, and pops of bold color.

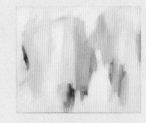

traditional

Stained wood, brass lanterns, and potted orchids.

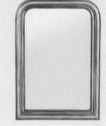

new country

Limed oak, leather-wrapped mirror, and simple stripes.

BE HONEST ABOUT
YOUR LIFESTYLE AND STUFF

Think long and hard about what you have in your hands when you enter and leave the house. You need to make sure those items have a place to live or else they will end up strewn everywhere, stressing you out. Then focus on making the functional elements as stylish as you can. For example, if you need tons of open shelving for all the accoutrements that come with kids and their activities, baskets or bins can contain the mess and be less visually (and mentally) stressful. Find a gorgeous big tray or dish for keys, change, and various small items. A drop-dead mirror can give you a last glance at your lipstick or outfit while also adding a bit of light and drama.

OPPOSITE: In this home the front door dead-ends into a coat closet, so the entry console table is off to the side in the living room. No need to apologize for this encroachment into the next room, though. By keeping it tidy and placing large art above, it blends in and serves many purposes.

ABOVE: A grass-cloth-covered tray is the perfect spot to drop keys and mail while keeping these little details contained and organized.

In this city condo, the homeowner had no built-in storage space whatsoever. We used a stylish dresser (*opposite*) as a place for her to store shoes, scarves, bags, and tons of other goods. Across the room we tucked another closed-door console (*above*) under the stairs for even more space to conceal clutter.

DARE TO ADD DRAMA

When it comes to walls and ceilings, think about what feeling you want to convey—soothing and serene with a calming paint color, or a bold statement with a lacquered, brightly colored ceiling or fabulous printed wallpaper. This is a great space to have fun, whatever your style or size of home, so don't be afraid to go a little crazy. It all depends on your level of comfort with pattern and color, but a good rule of thumb is that if you have a busy print on the walls, keep the rugs mostly solid and vice versa. Some people can totally live with busy pattern-on-pattern schemes, but if you are a decorating novice, going easier on the drama is a good guideline to follow.

OPPOSITE: This wide-open entry employs both detailed wallpaper and a statement rug to give it style. The round entry table is a perfect spot to display flowers when entertaining, making a great first impression for guests.

OPPOSITE: In this grand entryway of a family home, I wanted to mix several textures to create a warm, welcoming, but slightly formal look. The concrete-base table with a handmade wood top gives the homeowner a place to unload, and the leather and metal bench is a place to sit and take off shoes. An iron and rock crystal lantern adds a dash of "fancy," as does the large-scale modern art and vintage overdyed Persian rug. The walls are painted in Farrow & Ball Skimming Stone.

LEFT AND ABOVE: Leading into this space is a vestibule area, which we painted a soothing and dramatic deep gray and used basket-weave Carrara marble tile with a Greek key border to dress up the floor and relate to patterns found inside the home. A statement knocker sets the tone.

RIGHT: While this condo (in an old church) is huge, there is no dedicated entry. We created a small "moment" by the front door with a bold-colored small console placed in front of a floor mirror. This distinguishes the space from the open-plan living area.

OPPOSITE: This was the entry of a rental apartment we lived in years ago. One wall had copious amounts of hooks for all our coats and bags, while the other had an attractive little console table, antique mirror, and stack of vintage suitcases that stored our seasonal cold-weather gear!

STYLISH STORAGE IDEAS AND DÉCOR DETAILS

Most people will have a coat closet by the front door to conceal outerwear, but if you don't (like me), consider finding great-looking hooks that will add to the character of your design, even when they are empty. Also, pick a rug that you aren't afraid to wipe your feet on but that also adds something to the décor—not just a boring, tiny entry mat. Indoor/outdoor area rugs work wonders in this application! If you have the room for it, there is no better place for statement lighting—be it a chandelier or a lip-quiveringly good table lamp on a console. If your entry is more formal than utilitarian, consider a console with two x-benches underneath. It's one of my favorite looks and is a great way to introduce some fabric into the space and give people a place to sit and put on shoes!

renter's tip

You don't need to put big nail holes in the wall to have an entry mirror—lean a tall wall mirror behind a slim, small console (as shown above) to create a cool, layered look that also functions well.

In this small city entry, metallic wallpaper creates a glamorous statement, with deep-green walls and framed botanical prints to break up the pattern. A bound sisal remnant not only fits the space perfectly but can also take a beating from foot traffic.

In this narrow Beacon Hill town house, the entry level had no coat closet. So we designed a built-in wall unit beneath the stairs containing a closet, drawers, and cabinets to store every possible item for a young family.

OPPOSITE: With the open stairwell, there wasn't a lot of wall space for us to play with, so we leaned a dramatic piece of art atop the console to complete the look. Below, we tucked in two custom-upholstered x-benches that can be pulled into the adjoining living room for additional seating.

ABOVE: In this Chicago town house, we wanted the entry to really make a statement. We paired a refurbished vintage console with two amazing malachite-print-upholstered stools and hung a glamorous crystal-and-brass pendant. The large window is dressed in a linen Roman shade banded with wide tape trim.

In this grand home, the entry encompasses many spaces, from a cozy window seat with custom cushions and Roman shade to the chest of drawers that serves as a console. But the real drama is in the silver-leafed lantern that hangs in the stairwell.

COASTERS & A GREAT
BOTTLE OF WINE

A PERSONALIZED NEW DOORMAT

10 GREAT
HOUSEWARMING GIFTS

Personalization makes any gift that much more special. Create
custom pairings of goodies aligned with your host's hobbies or
interests. When time allows, have something monogrammed to
really make yourself stand out as a thoughtful visitor!

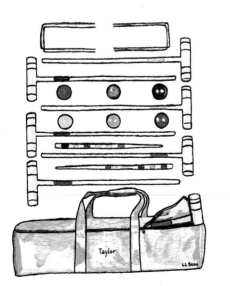

OUTDOOR GAME SET

GOURMET TREATS THEY'LL ACTUALLY EAT!

A COOKBOOK & FAVORITE
KITCHEN TOOLS

RETURN ADDRESS STAMP

MONOGRAMMED MATCHES &
A DELIGHTFUL CANDLE

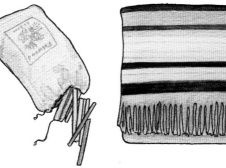

FIRESTARTERS &
A COZY BLANKET

TERRARIUMS INSTEAD
OF FLOWERS

A MONOGRAMMED
MODERN TRAY

THE LIVING ROOM

THE HONEST TRUTH
ABOUT BEING A DESIGNER

The most common misconception about being an interior designer is that it's consistently glamorous and a rockin' good time. People assume that we spend all day picking out fabrics and gorgeous furniture and spending piles of money. I am here to tell you that no matter what it looks like in the glossy pages of magazines, this is absolutely NOT the case. There is so much more behind those perfect rooms you see, and it ain't always pretty.

I went into this business because of my pure passion and undeniable designer DNA. Not as in "my parents had me made in a test tube of only the good chromosomes," but, rather, I felt that art and design were in my blood. My father is a self-taught "architectural

OPPOSITE: This is the corner of the couch where I write my blog each day. The burl wood side tables were handmade specifically to coordinate with the higher arm of the sofa.

designer" (we can't say architect because he never spent a day in a classroom for it, but for all intents and purposes he is one). Having found that he needed to work in the family business (a women's clothing store—more on that later), he took to books to feed his passion for architecture and design. As he maintained his role in the store, he began designing a few projects on the side, from garages to small homes. Over the years his self-taught design practice grew (with the help of a licensed architect or two, of course) giving him the opportunity to make the business his full-time occupation. And eventually this self-made man beat out other big-city firms to land a game-changing job designing one of the biggest casinos in the world. To say I'm proud is the understatement of the year.

I spent my formative years drawing floor plans and playing with fabric swatches. It is the smell of blueprints, not Play-Doh, that takes me back to being a kid, even now. When I got older, I decided I wanted to go into interior design, which seemed to blend my love of beautiful things with my interest in the structure of gorgeous homes, like those my father builds. I saw myself as picking up where he leaves off, if you will (even though he likes to be a part of the entire process right down to what kind of grass is planted, like any good control-freak creative type!). Until I started working in design, though, I thought, like you probably do,

that this must be the most fabulous, stress-free job there is!

The truth is, it is fabulous. But stress free? That's laughable. Spending other people's money is fun, but with it comes a boatload of responsibility and pressure. Typically you learn this lesson the hard way—with a very expensive mistake. Early on in my career I had selected these fabulous lanterns for a client's hallway that cost a FORTUNE. I was so enamored with them and her house that I managed to overlook the fact that I needed to double-check whether or not they would work with her ceiling height. When they came in and I got the call from my client that her fancy lanterns would smack her in the head if she hung them, I thought I was going to be sick right there in my car.

Happily I was able to rectify the situation thanks to a very kind vendor and some replacement fixtures of the right size, but I did end up losing some money along with some confidence in myself. And there have been many nights that I have woken up in a cold sweat with the panicky, heart attack–like feeling that I ordered the wrong size sofa for someone. There are so many details that go into the

OPPOSITE: I fell madly in love with this blue-and-white chinoiserie vase and paid no mind to the old adage never to mix blue and black. It adds such a great graphic quality to the space.

process of design—minute, nitpicky, math-related kinds of things (which is funny because I am a big-picture, barely-passed-fundamentals-of-precalculus type of girl). But, like my dad, I have surrounded myself with people who have talents I don't to comprise a winning team—people who are amazing at organizing, paperwork (there is TONS of it), and double-checking details. I remain a big-picture gal. I know that is what I am best at. You have to know your strengths and admit your weaknesses in order to be really good at what you do.

You also need a level head and patience to make it in this business, qualities that don't come naturally to me, but I have learned to muster up time and time again, making me a much nicer, slightly saner person. There are clients for whom nothing is ever right, there are some who want everything yesterday, no excuses, and others who will go around your back and order something direct from a vendor, cutting you out of your commission. There are manufacturers who do not care that your very important client needs a table in time for Thanksgiving and aren't even sorry they are running sixteen weeks behind schedule! As a designer, you have to manage these issues every single day—playing the middleman, the negotiator, and the psychiatrist all at the same time. But for every issue that arises and every client that makes you cry, there are a bunch of engaging, awesome people that look at you with gratitude and say, "Thank you so much for making my house so beautiful."

And while I am adept at advising others on what sofas to put in their living rooms, designing my own home is my Achilles' heel. It's a common complaint in the industry, as we have the luxury and the agony of knowing that something better will come out RIGHT when you finally place an order. So my home is continually in progress—when one room's paint is drying, I'm already picking out my NEW favorite color. Never mind the little details like bedding and pillows! My husband will come in the house and ask what happened to all our new pillows, to which I'll respond, "Those were OLD pillows, silly man (three months old, in fact), and these are our NEW fabulous pillows!" Of course even those end up in the basement or for sale on the blog within three more months. I am my own worst client: the one who can never make a decision, second-guesses everything, doesn't want to spend a fortune for the good stuff, and changes her mind the SECOND anything is delivered.

A good example is our sofa. Or, should I say, sofas. When we moved into the house, we brought with us the navy velvet beauty I swore to Andrew was "the sofa to end all sofas." Well, after about a week in the house I decided that Navy Sofa needed to go live with a nice new family on a farm. I wanted a gray sofa, because that was the direction this house was going—monochromatic! Very chic! Not blue! (said with dramatic waving-hand gestures to accentuate my point). So after hemming and hawing over which one would be right, I ordered a new gray sectional. We waited and waited and spent uncomfortable nights watching *Will & Grace* reruns on our tiny, uncomfortable sunroom sofa because Navy Sofa moved to a mansion in a fancier suburb (way to go, Navy Sofa!). When the new sofa arrived, I was dancing around like it was Christmas morning and I was a seven-year-old child. But my stomach dropped as they set it up. It was the wrong orientation. The stupid chaise was on the wrong side. Fearing that I had made another classic miscalculation, I checked my paperwork and was relieved to see that I had ordered it correctly; it was the furniture company that had messed up. And due to that, I was going to get a replacement for a song.

More uncomfortable movie nights took place and then finally it arrived, in the correct orientation and everything, and guess what? I hated it. Like, hated it. All the research and planning and storyboarding in the world will not keep you (or me) from disliking something when it finally is in the space. So after we found yet another home for Gray Sofa (and began feeling like the Unloved Sofa Rescue League) we finally got it right. I ordered the sofa I had loved from the beginning but wasn't ready to spend the money on. A very well-made piece done in a fabric of my choosing made gorgeous by tufting and nailhead trim and crafted to the exact proportions of my space. Had I listened to my gut and just ordered it in the first place, I would have avoided a lot of hassle, wasted money, and emotional distress worrying about finding former sofas loving new homes.

So, see, even those of us who do this for a living suffer from the same decorating afflictions everyone else does—bad purchases, regrets, miscalculations, and fear. But the benefit of having one of us on your side through the process is that we've made many more mistakes than you and learned a lot from them. Life always seems to work that way—you've gotta get your hands dirty and fall on your face a few times in order to come out the other side smarter, stronger, and ready to pick the right sofa.

LIFE ALWAYS SEEMS TO WORK THAT WAY—YOU'VE GOTTA GET YOUR HANDS DIRTY AND FALL ON YOUR FACE A FEW TIMES IN ORDER TO COME OUT THE OTHER SIDE SMARTER, STRONGER, AND READY TO PICK THE RIGHT SOFA.

12 BEST
SOFA STYLES

CHESTERFIELD

MID-CENTURY MODERN

ENGLISH ROLL ARM

LOOSE BACK

TUXEDO

TRADITIONAL SLIPCOVER

Here is a cheat sheet to the twelve best sofa styles that I believe will stand the test of time. When selecting this most important piece for a living room, it's best to err on the side of classic and neutral. If you desire to make a statement, it's best left to pillows and accent chairs as they are much easier (and less costly) to change.

LOUIS STYLE

MODERN TUFTED

MODERN SLIPCOVER

SWOOP ARM

MODERN WOOD FRAME

CAMELBACK

OPPOSITE: This vintage buffet was an estate sale find for $75. It acts as a bar and cleverly hides all our cable boxes and components. We positioned holes to run wires so that the doors don't have to be open. The walls are painted in Benjamin Moore Balboa Mist.

LEFT: We call her Our Lady of the Bar, and she's a replica found online—no real marble here! Occasionally I like adorning her in jewelry to add some interest (and humor).

LAYING OUT THE LIVING ROOM

In our house the living room has to be a place we can formally entertain as well as kick back and relax, as currently it's the ONLY living space we have in the house. Whether you have a separate formal space or an all-in-one situation like me, there are some basic tips that will help you create a space of your dreams with a style that you won't get sick of.

While our living room is small, we've utilized the space to work for our family. The sectional allows us both to lounge comfortably while the glass coffee table keeps the room from feeling cramped.

CLOCKWISE, FROM TOP LEFT: The throw pillows on the sofa are a mix of textures and patterns, from a printed linen to a soft velvet trimmed in Greek key tape to a striped woven wool. I like just a *touch* of color, and this provides that punch for me. • The brass-framed coffee table is topped with coordinating accessories. A fragrant candle is the most important addition to a cozy space. • The interior of the cabinets in the bar have had MANY different looks over the years, from the original canary yellow, to turquoise, then Hermès orange, and now papered in a malachite wall covering. It's an easy way to make an old piece work in various spaces.

OPPOSITE: A quiet corner anchored by my favorite Mitchell Gold + Bob Williams chair in a worn saddle leather. Paired with an Ikea lamp and marble-top tulip table, it's the perfect little corner for reading.

LEFT: In this grand New York living room, we wanted to keep things modern and monochromatic yet fun. A striped Calvin Klein fabric on the sofa is an unexpected touch, and the large horse photograph, printed on a Lucite panel, acts as a focal point.

ABOVE: The opposite corner of the same living room holds a silver-leafed bookcase full of little objects the clients have collected over time. The walls are painted in Farrow & Ball Elephant's Breath.

OVERLEAF LEFT TO RIGHT: A grand, paneled Back Bay library serves as both a formal living room and an office for our client. We made some bold choices with a purple overdyed rug, shagreen-wrapped modern desk, and mirrored side table. • These Kravet benches are among my favorite items I ever designed—the marbleized fabric looks so incredible in this application and provides that wow factor!

ANCHOR IT

When it comes to rugs, the bigger the better! Make sure your rug is big enough to anchor the room and the furniture within it. A rule of thumb is that at least two legs of all the main furniture should rest on the rug. Of course, there are room sizes and shapes that make this impossible, but please avoid the "rug island" look, where only the coffee table sits on top and no other furniture touches it! Nothing makes a space look smaller or more unfinished than that type of setup. If you find a rug you love but it's not big enough for your space, layer it over a larger simple sisal for a bohemian, modern look!

OPPOSITE: We really drew attention to the ceiling and height of this room by using graphic tones of tans and browns with green accents.

ABOVE, LEFT TO RIGHT: We dressed up this custom-skirted side table with a bold emerald-green lamp and hints of gold. • The recesses of the coffered ceiling were papered in a chocolate-brown grass cloth. A large fabric pendant provides illumination and drama.

THE LARGE AND SMALL OF IT

No matter the actual physical size of your living room, you want it to feel cozy, welcoming, and well proportioned. To make a smaller room feel bigger, consider painting the walls a dark shade to make the corners recede, and make sure your area rug is large enough to cover most of the floor. Using fewer, larger-scale furniture pieces can really make the room feel more welcoming than a clutter of smaller furniture. For large rooms that lack intimacy, create a couple of seating areas that feel more intimate than one massive one that leaves you ten feet away from the nearest person.

A PRIVILEGED LIFE
PARIS HOTEL STORI

OPPOSITE: This condo is actually in a renovated old church and thankfully some of the original details remain. We dressed them up with custom mirrors and library sconces. A commissioned Amanda Talley painting brings some color up onto the wall.

ABOVE RIGHT: Adding books, art, and objects to a deep mantel makes it more interesting. Layering is your friend here!

ABOVE: In this living room we added pops of bright yellow to bring in some attitude while maintaining the modern-meets-traditional aesthetic. The walls are painted in Benjamin Moore Revere Pewter.

ABOVE: A large-scale abstract painting works well with a velvet-upholstered modern wingback chair. Hints of brass and the textured shag rug warm up the space.

PILLOW FIGHT

I prefer to use nice oversized pillows on the sofa. For a smaller-scale sofa, like a love seat or "apartment" size, I like twenty-inch squares. For larger sofas and sectionals twenty-two- to twenty-four-inch squares work best. For most chairs eighteen-inch squares or lumbar shapes fit perfectly. Down inserts always look and feel more luxe and less stiff than foam fillers.

ABOVE, LEFT TO RIGHT: A great example of mixing patterns: a wide stripe, geometric print, and fuzzy texture all work so nicely together. • This enormous sectional provides ample seating for entertaining while still looking sleek. The custom-designed coffee table introduces a new texture and is stained a coordinating dark gray tone.

OPPOSITE: A bolder palette was employed to decorate this home—a spacious condominium in a converted church. One of the coolest spaces I've had the pleasure to work on!

OPPOSITE: Pops of icy blue liven up this rather neutral living space, while a Lucite-and-brass bookcase provides the glamour.

LEFT: Bold colors reign in this suburban home—from the pillows to the lamps to the drop-dead gorgeous lilacs!

MIX AND MATCH

Everyone has a different tolerance for mixing patterns. Some people like the cacophony of an eclectic and busy mix; others prefer something more calming. A safe rule of thumb: in one room you can mix one geometric pattern, one small scale or stripe, and one organic (floral, paisley, etc.) among your rugs, upholstery, pillows, and drapes. Please, please don't use three geometric patterns in one room.

CURTAIN CALL

The size and width of drapes depends on the size of window you are dressing—for single bay windows single-width drapes are fine, but when dealing with multibay or extra-wide windows, you'll need to use double-width drapes to properly close and balance the scale of the window to the fabric when open. I love the look of woven-wood Roman shades layered underneath drapery, as it creates a truly cozy, textural look while also being functional. And make sure that all window treatments in your home that are visible from the exterior of the house are lined in white to create a seamless look from the outside!

ABOVE: High ceilings in this condo were emphasized by custom drapes, while the slightly awkward room shape is made cozy with the help of small chairs and a deep sofa.

OPPOSITE: The clients brought this unique, curved sectional with them from Manhattan to their new formal living room in their Beacon Hill town house. We paired it with a wingback chair upholstered in a fantastic leaf print and drapes in an ikat stripe to add color. The walls are painted in Farrow & Ball Cornforth White.

OVERLEAF: A pair of small-scale wingback chairs provide seating and a special little vignette in the space. Tall silk drapes add softness. A custom Amanda Talley drawing above the historic marble fireplace creates quite a statement. The walls are Benjamin Moore Metro Gray.

OPPOSITE: We created a gallery wall using some meaningful artwork and a resin deer head above a tufted sofa.

LEFT: Bold blue lamps sit atop a lacquer console table, providing color and light in this living room.

LEVELS OF LIGHT

The way a room is lit can make or break the style and mood. Do not rely on one type of lighting alone—just because you have fifteen recessed can lights doesn't mean you don't need others! Break it up by mixing table or floor lamps with ceiling fixtures or sconces. And please install dimmers where possible to allow you to adjust the brightness of certain fixtures. Custom lampshades also help dress up vintage or bargain store finds to look uniquely yours. I've added grosgrain ribbon onto many a plain white shade for a little special touch. Get out your glue guns!

TAPE IT OUT

When deciding on furniture for a room, I like to advise clients to use painter's tape to tape out the scale of a large piece like a sofa or armoire on the floor or wall to REALLY get a sense of the space it will take up in the room.

ABOVE: Fun pops of color atop the bar.

OPPOSITE: Our vintage buffet in one of its previous incarnations—orange! Flanked by our favorite Sapien bookshelves, we created a little dedicated area in our open-plan living and kitchen level.

THE COFFEE TABLE CONUNDRUM

Glass versus wood? Oval versus square? Your coffee-table selection has a lot to do with your lifestyle: materials, shape, and size all depend on your household (kids and glass don't mix well) and your room (big leather ottoman-style tables eat up a small space). A good rule of thumb is that there should be an 18-inch space between the sofa or other seating and the table. And don't overlook grouping a few small tables together to create a unique, multipurpose "coffee table."

OPPOSITE: This trunk, found at a discount store, served as our coffee table and garnered many compliments!

ABOVE: In a previous apartment of mine, I went bold with a navy velvet sofa and hints of coral pink.

ABOVE: The first room of mine ever published was the living room in my old condo. It looks dated to me now, but still works because of the clean lines, traditional shapes, and fabrics. The walls are painted in Benjamin Moore Manchester Tan.

OPPOSITE: A dark-brown accent wall creates drama in a city loft. Traditional artwork hung in a grid really pops off the dark background, while the modern geometric rug contrasts nicely.

renter's tip

When selecting new furniture, stick to pieces that are flexible and not specific to your current space. A large sectional that fits a large loft won't work in a smaller brownstone apartment (trust me, I had this issue). Stick to standard-width sofas (86 inches or less), individual chairs, and accent tables that can be used in ANY size or shape space.

MAKING PRETTY PICTURES

I learned early on in this business that design magazines are like fashion magazines. The reality of what is being photographed is far from the perfect image you see on the page. Staging, cropping, lighting, Photoshop, and a near-hysterical designer are involved in every single picture. So don't feel bad when you see these homes with everything just so; they were only like that for a day. Here is an example of what it takes to get those amazing, perfect shots:

DAY 1: A real magazine wants to shoot my project! I am a grown-up, legitimate designer! This is magnificent news, worthy of three or four drinks! Cheers to me! I have so much time to prepare!

DAY 3: Holy sh*t, this is happening in two weeks! I need to start gathering supplies. I just remembered that the client never ordered a coffee table AND I'm pretty sure the pillows have been destroyed by the kids. Do I have time to make new ones?

DAY 4: Every fabric I want to use is back-ordered eighty-two weeks. I'm screwed.

DAY 5: Drive to Target, HomeGoods, flower market, and design center looking for accessories and loaner furniture. Find nothing. Repeat daily for a week.

DAY 6: Find out that there are no books in any of the bookshelves and I will have to fill them completely. Will anyone notice my Twilight series stuck in there?

DAY 6: My sixteenth trip to HomeGoods. The store manager contemplates a shopping addiction intervention. I start muttering to myself in the aisles, things like, "Why aren't there any turquoise foo dogs here? WHY?!?!"

OPPOSITE: The patterned drapes frame a pair of widely matted prints in gold frames atop an antiqued mirror console. The small-scale leopard-print chairs add just a dash of whimsy.

DAY 7: Pay a million dollars to overnight ship a bunch of accessories. Sorry, bank account.

DAY 8: The rug I ordered for the shoot is now not going to make it in time. Good thing I have one just like it in my own living room. Will have to get wine and spaghetti stains out of it ASAP.

DAY 8: "Clients? What clients?"

DAY 9: Facebook friends become concerned about negative, homicidal status updates. Husband contemplates a straitjacket as birthday gift this year. I request that it's at least leopard and monogrammed.

DAY 9: Wake up in the middle of the night screaming things like "white hydrangeas," "brass napkin rings," and "deer antlers."

DAY 10: Text/call assistant on her day off, obsessively. Cry a lot.

DAY 11: Make husband and assistant assemble random Ikea items. Dodge their evil glares like a ninja.

DAY 12: Select six different paintings for the living room. Must have options. Car is full to the sunroof with stuff and husband is wondering where all his books have gone.

SHOOT DAY!

5:15 A.M.: Up before roosters! Arrive at the flower market and buy every single bloom in the joint due to indecision. It looks like we are about to open a mobile florist shop in the parking lot.

8:00 A.M.: Have incredible trouble picking out a houseplant. Feels equivalent to finding peace in the Middle East. Stress has reduced my brain to Jell-O.

9:00 A.M.: Shoot starts in forty-five minutes but I am not liking that silver vase one bit. Send assistant to speed to the store to get a new one. She probably updates her résumé in the car and/or contemplates driving into road divider.

9:15 A.M.: Carry thirty-seven loads of heavy boxes, flowers, accessories, and art into the house. Grab kitchen shears and start hacking at flowers in effort to make some kind of arrangement.

9:30 A.M.: Photographers arrive. Go around unplugging every light and taping the cords to things so they don't show. Walk around yelling, "No wires or cords!" like Mommie Dearest.

10:00 A.M.: Have to hang a massive borrowed painting on the wall without making any holes. Finagle seven sticky

hooks to do the job. Decide those sticky-hook inventors should get the Nobel Prize.

10:18 A.M.: Room is the wrong orientation. Shot needs to be vertical. Room is horizontal. Basically write out mathematical theorem trying to figure out how to make it work.

11:00 A.M.: Click. Click. Click.

11:00 A.M.–2:00 P.M.: Run up the stairs. Run down the stairs. Repeat three hundred times.

2:00 P.M.: Think about celebratory dinner husband has surely planned. Click. Click.

2:10 P.M.: Argue with photographer about angles. Shift furniture into bizarre configuration that looks great through the lens but like a blind person arranged it in real life.

3:00 P.M.: WE FORGOT WHITE HY-DRANGEAS!! Try to find paper bag to breathe into.

4:00 P.M.: Last shot.

4:01 P.M.: I forgot we have to move everything out and take everything down we've added to the rooms. My quads ache at the thought.

5:30 P.M.: Home. Husband did NOT plan celebratory dinner. Hmph. Ryan Gosling surely would have.

6:00 P.M.: Go out for dinner. Eat entire large pizza. Pat self on back.

8:45 P.M.: Go to bed same time as most toddlers. Dream of wild editorial success (and Ryan Gosling).

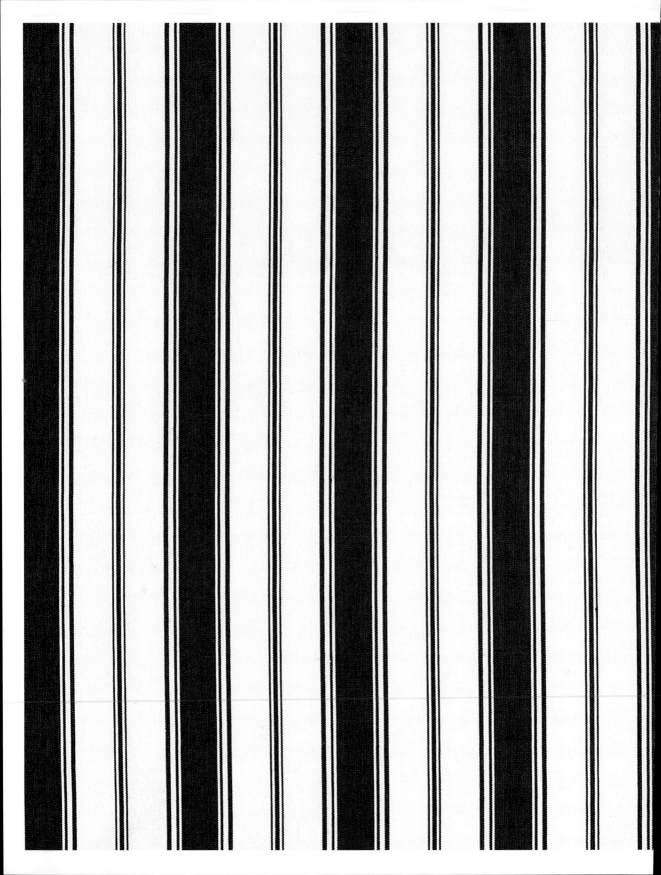

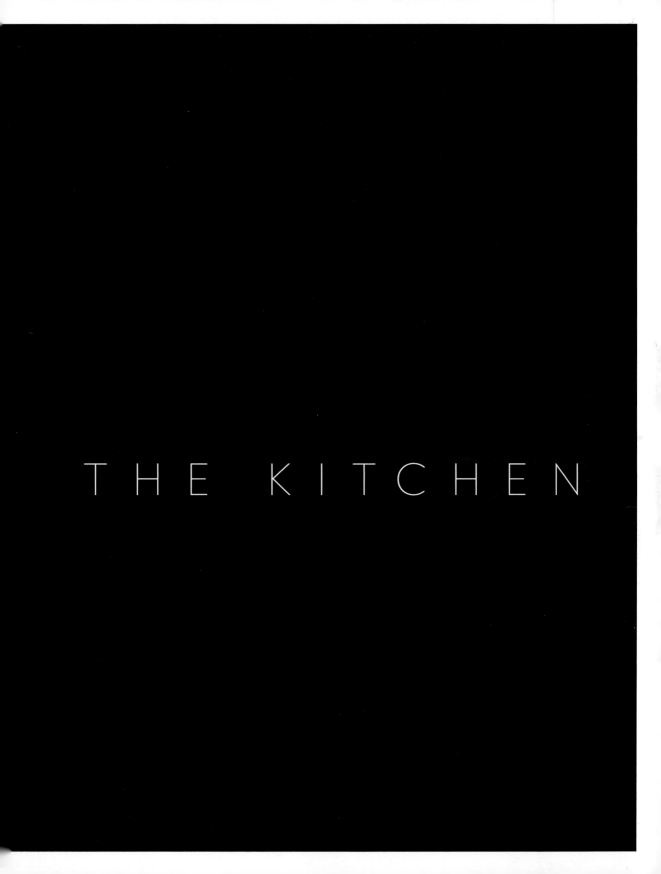

THE KITCHEN

SURVIVING A
KITCHEN RENOVATION

Hey Erin . . . we've got a little problem. Call me as soon as you can . . ." Click.

And just like that, my sunny Aruba-induced bliss was shattered by the stomach-churning anxiety of my renovation. My brain went to the deepest, darkest places it could. What was going on? Did my house collapse onto itself (a constant fear of mine, even as insane as it was)? Did they discover it was rotting from the inside and needed to be totally razed? Perhaps they found an infestation of termites in the walls? I knew it was a bad idea to go on vacation during the demolition phase of construction, but my dear, sweet husband thought it would be a great way to escape

OPPOSITE: My kitchen after the renovation. While I absolutely LOVE it, I, of course, have a few things I would change. The lower cabinets are painted in Benjamin Moore Cape May Cobblestone.

the noise and dust. Why did I listen to him? I needed to be there to micromanage this whole disaster—leaving such a big project in others' hands is the stuff my control-freak nightmares are crafted of!

No matter who you are or WHERE you are, a message like that is the LAST thing you want to hear. During our six-week renovation, every time my phone rang and my contractor's number flashed onto the screen my heart would stop. I developed a bit of a Pavlovian response, knowing that most of the time the only reason he called was to convey bad news or tell me he needed more money. But if you've ever renovated anything, you know that call will come (most likely again and again) and typically at the most inopportune time. Like while you are sunbathing or feeling deliriously happy.

The "little problem" in the message I got at the beach was our dear friend asbestos. And the cost of remedying this "little problem" was a big bill of $3,000. Welcome to my kitchen renovation, everyone. Where anxiety is the norm and waterproof mascara is a necessity. Because let me tell you, no matter HOW easy it may seem at the outset, you will be crying at some point. All the tears are worth it, and so is the money most of the time, but it is a process rife with stress that even those of us who do this for a living are susceptible to. Perhaps even more.

When we bought our house, I declared that I could NOT live in our kitchen for more than a month without renovating it. The classic, i.e., disgusting, 1950s original space contained stained laminate counters, a greasy old electric range, creaky cabinets that smelled like a funeral home, and NO DISHWASHER OR DISPOSAL. Now, I can get down with an old stove (mostly by not using it at all and instead ordering in), but having to hand wash a pile of gross dishes after a big meal was so not my jam. And there's really nothing like trying to catch soggy dog food chunks from going down the drain after a mindless rinse to light a fire under your ass to get a move on with home improvement. Seeing as our first set of renovations (which were even MORE pressing considering the spine-tingling state of our one full bathroom) went over budget, we had to wait a few months. Until we could take it no longer. And by we, I mean me, because my husband seemed to think it was okeydokey except for the small fridge.

MEN.

I declared that I didn't care how much it cost, we were renovating the damn kitchen. Being in the design industry, I get pretty great pricing on materials and got to exchange hugs for architectural drawings thanks to my father's handy-dandy "owning an architectural firm" thing. How expensive could it be? We were just taking down some walls, demolishing everything in sight, and starting completely from scratch! Piece. Of. Cake.

Did I mention we set out to do all this in January? In New England? Yes, I am a bona fide GENIUS. No grill to cook on, foot upon foot of snow (i.e., delays), zero insulation, and super-fun amounts of cold air rushing into the house! There is nothing more soul crushing than having to shovel out two feet of snow from a blizzard only to come inside and have no kitchen, no walls, no lights, sawdust everywhere, and only a stale bag of pretzels to eat. We became such good friends with the pizza guy that sometimes he would look at us in pity when we answered the door, as if to say, *Really? Three times this week? You guys are worse than college stoners.*

Before all this began, however, Andrew and I (and our architect, my dad) each had different ideas about how the space should look and function. Luckily, they were close enough that we came to an agreed-upon layout we all liked rather quickly. I deferred on points regarding construction and function to my dad's expertise in these areas and pushed back when I knew my aesthetic and his would never jive. Andrew and I have a bit more of a modern streak than my dad, and I knew I had to stay true to that while respecting his invaluable experience in this arena.

Dad's knowledge was very valuable when it came to my cabinets. He recommended a great vendor, whom I used, but he didn't necessarily agree on my obsession with gray cabinets. Especially the two-tone application I had in mind with white uppers and gray lowers. Since buying this house, my mantra about the kitchen was simply "gray lowers, white uppers." I swear, I'd wake up from dreams muttering that phrase. We picked a simple Shaker-style overlay door and drawer (insets would have been nice, but man oh man, so much more money!). I quickly picked a white for the upper cabinets, but then I had to choose the custom gray color for the lower cabinets. And opened up a Pandora's box.

Since our old cabinets were going to be ripped out, I tested paint samples right on them. I picked out three colors thinking one would be the clear winner. I'm pretty much a color ninja, but once they went up, I had no clue. I wanted a medium, slightly warm gray. But one was too dark, one too green, and one too purple. So I went to get more—one too brown, one too blue, and another too tan. I had become the Goldilocks of gray! I went back again, and again and again, until it looked like our kitchen had been attacked by some lunatic doing a weird installation art piece entitled *Indecisive Designer*. I swear, after the third email telling me they needed my decision about color or else the cabinet delivery would be held up, I was rocking back and forth on the floor like Rain Man muttering the color names under my breath. I posted pictures to Twitter, Instagram, and the blog asking readers to help me choose and of course got back a completely evenly divided response. Blerg.

I finally narrowed it down to two finalists and asked Andrew his opinion. This is how it went:

ME: *Which color do you like best?*

ANDREW: *Those aren't different colors; they are the same.*

ME: *Oh my God, no they aren't, the left is way bluer and the right way greener! Are you blind??*

ANDREW: *I don't even like gray.*

ME: *I hate you.*

No help from him. And knowing me, had he picked one, I would have gone with the other. It's how I tend to roll in our marriage, and yes, I will talk to my therapist about that. I got so frustrated with myself that I finally just picked one shade willy-nilly and sent it off to the cabinet maker. And then I lost ALL hope for sleep for the next few weeks awaiting their arrival and having nightmares that they would be purple.

And then in the middle of demolition and the initial build-out, I got the flu. Really bad. And if you think living through a kitchen renovation is torture, try doing it while deathly ill and stuck in bed while the sound of pipe cutters and hammers assaults your ears for eight hours a day and there are strange men wandering inside your destroyed house. It's also fun when they have to shut off the water to the one bathroom you can make it to out of their line of vision and instead have to use the one downstairs in the middle of the fray. I am pretty sure the crew was quite impressed with my palm-leaf print pajamas and bed-head hair. I was so miserable, I took an air mattress into my studio and slept on the floor there while dictating design decisions (and my will) to my assistant from my deathbed.

Once back in the land of the living, I had so many other details to ponder, like countertops and hardware. My whole life, all I wanted for my dream kitchen was Carrara marble counters with my gray cabinets. My dad said marble would be a nightmare and stained too much. I said I didn't care. Andrew pointed out to me how much of a pain in the ass our Carrara counter in our bathroom was. I didn't care—I was getting my damn marble counters in my kitchen! Then Andrew showed me

CLOCKWISE FROM ABOVE LEFT: Everything has its place in this small space—a wine rack, microwave, and nice big farm sink included! And we can't forget the coffee machine, a total must. • I decided to mix metals and use brass hardware instead of nickel or chrome. I think it adds a lovely richness when paired with the stone and gray cabinets. • We splurged on a nice stove and hood, as it's a focal point in the space. The subway tile, however, was a bargain!

a ring left on the bathroom counter by a soap dispenser and brought up my love for red wine and loathing of cleaning up after myself. I finally agreed that if I could find something I liked as much that was more durable, it might be a good idea.

After much research, I actually did find something better—a quartzite called Bianco Macaubas that is harder than granite and even more gorgeous than my beloved marble. I read all sorts of great things about it on various renovation forums (if it's on the internet, it has to be true) and so I went to go see some slabs. When my assistant and I went into the stone yard, we were given a guide that illustrated the pricing structure: one star meant affordable and it went up and up to five stars, which meant you will have to sell some organs for this stone unless you are Beyoncé. We found my slabs, I yelped in absolute glee, and then saw that it was like a friggin' constellation of stars on the label. I shook my fist at the sky and (internally) yelled, *Damn you good taste, DAMN YOU!* while wondering which organ I maybe could do without. I do have *two* kidneys. . . .

But when it came down to it, our kitchen was small and we only needed 50 square feet to do the whole thing. And since Andrew said absolutely, 100 percent, over his dead body could I do Carrara marble, I knew I would not be happy with anything else. So we ponied up

some savings and went for it. And once my cabinets came in (in a wonderful shade of gray, thank goodness) I knew everything was going to come together perfectly. And then the day the magical counters were installed, I got a text from my contractor with a picture of them. And almost died. They looked darker than I remembered and had HUGE stains on them! I rushed home in a complete panic and practically jumped out of the car while it was still moving to get into the house as fast as I could to see them.

They looked better in person but were still covered in stains! My fingers could not dial the stone company's number fast enough, and I may or may not have had a complete *Poltergeist*-style meltdown on the phone with some salesguy who barely spoke English. But he spoke enough to alert me to the fact that this was natural stone and they didn't guarantee ANYTHING. As my ugly-crying dissipated into calm rationalization, we came to find out that the stains were water from the water saw and that because this stone was SO hard, it had taken days to cut, which meant water had sat on them for a long time. They would dry, and they turned out to be the BEST choice for our kitchen, being both drop-dead gorgeous and insanely durable. Even against my copious wine spillage. Andrew tries hard not to say "I told you so" daily.

But the devil is in the details, and for me that meant hardware, tile, and lighting, the jewelry of the kitchen, so to speak. Cabinets, counters, and appliances are all pretty clean and simple in most homes, but the real style of the kitchen lies in the more decorative elements. Before we even knocked a wall down, I had my pendant lights and brass hardware picked out, but the whole "brass thing" was not a popular choice with the better half. After much cajoling and reasoning, he let me have my way—and the vision I had for my kitchen began coming to life right before my eyes. Eyes that have a very critical filter on them, which meant I became an insane person about the tiles of my backsplash. A budget friendly option for us, and one I loved, was simple white subway tile with dark gray grout. So classic and easy to take care of. This was it, the pièce de résistance! The crowning jewel to make this design complete! What could go wrong? I left instructions with the tile guy and went to work only to come home to tiles WAY closer together than I wanted and grout lines that left MUCH to be desired. Ask any of my high school math teachers and they will tell you I sucked at it, but all of a sudden I became a regular Einstein when it came to millimeters and measurements. Andrew said

BUT THE DEVIL IS IN THE DETAILS, AND FOR ME THAT MEANT HARDWARE, TILE, AND LIGHTING, THE JEWELRY OF THE KITCHEN, SO TO SPEAK.

he actually liked the skinny grout lines, and after seeing all the finishing touches complete, I had to agree. Sometimes there are happy accidents that mean the design gods are making moves to create something you didn't think you wanted.

The process was stressful but not a disaster, and now having lived through the process of dreaming, doubting, believing, and ultimately succeeding for myself, I am a better designer for others. I feel much more sympathy when something goes wrong or a decision feels like the end of the world. You spend a fortune on your house to begin with, so gutting it, ripping it to shreds, and starting anew from the bare bones is a traumatic and trying experience. You have to trust those you've chosen to work with and maintain your faith in the fact that it will all be worth it when it's done. I turned something I hated into something I adore. And now that I have this gorgeous kitchen, I suppose it's time to learn to cook better and not just use it to make grilled cheese and tacos from Old El Paso kits. My kitchen is a joy to spend time in, which is a good thing, because I am not doing this again ANYTIME soon.

DESIGNING YOUR DREAM KITCHEN

THE LAYOUT

GO WITH THE FLOW

The layout of your kitchen is so incredibly important. If your kitchen looks great but isn't functional, it will leave you frazzled, especially considering how much money kitchens cost to design. Existing plumbing can sometimes limit where you place your appliances

OPPOSITE: We knocked down a wall to open the kitchen up to the dining room, which created a more open feel despite its tiny size. The glass pendants don't disturb the line of sight and the white upper cabinets keep things bright.

before

and sink, but if you can, try to place the garbage close to the sink and the dishwasher to one side of the sink. This will make your work flow smooth when you are prepping and cleaning up after meals. It's also a good idea to create a clear "triangle" in your kitchen where one point of the triangle is the sink, one is the stove, and one is the refrigerator. You don't want to have to walk around a table or island every time you need something from the refrigerator while cooking.

THINK AHEAD

A personalized storage plan will be key to your effective kitchen design. Pull out all your dishes, pots, pans, utensils, and anything else you plan to store in the kitchen and make sure your new design incorporates a spot for everything. You may find out you need more drawers and less cabinets or vice versa! You don't want to be left holding a Swiffer and an armful of spatulas with nowhere to put them when your kitchen is complete.

THE CABINETS

THE POWER OF PAINT

Painting your existing cabinets can be much cheaper then replacing them. If they are in good shape but just not your style, a coat of glossy paint can transform your space. Having them professionally sprayed will result in the smoothest finish, but it does cost more than doing them yourself.

STARTING FRESH

Installing new cabinets is the most important investment in your kitchen, so if you go this route, be sure to pick the best quality you can afford. Good cabinets can last decades, and if you stick to clean, simple lines you'll never regret money spent on them. Hardware can easily be changed, and if you tire of white in five years, you can always paint them.

Minor changes made a BIG impact in this Beacon Hill kitchen. We painted the cabinets white, replaced the counters, removed the mirrored backsplash, and reoriented the island. And now it looks completely different!

before

OPPOSITE: Playing off the gray-green existing Viking range, we re-painted the woodwork on the other side of the kitchen in Farrow & Ball Pigeon. New striped cushions on the banquette and a couple of bamboo chairs make the space comfortable and useful.

STICKING TO A BUDGET

Many times custom or semicustom cabinetry isn't in the cards due to budget constraints. Big box stores like Ikea, Lowe's, and Home Depot all offer fantastic options at a lower price point. Go to the store armed with ideas, pictures, measurements, and the plan for your space and find an associate you feel comfortable with. I've seen some truly stunning kitchens done through stores like these, so don't count them out!

OPEN SHELVING

I absolutely ADORE the look of open shelving in place of upper cabinets, but you have to be prepared to live with the reality of them. Dust collects easily on open shelves, so be ready to dust a lot and only store things on them that you use often. And speaking of the items you store on them, since they are always on display, make sure they are pretty and match! You won't be happy staring at your collection of mismatched coffee mugs all the time.

GLASS DOORS

Pay similar attention to detail if you are planning to use glass-front cabinets. Your finer, more decorative china, glassware, and serveware should be stored in glass-front cabinets. If you plan to install interior cabinet lighting, use glass shelves so that the light shines through the entire cabinet, not just on the top shelf!

THE COUNTERS

Be honest about your lifestyle when picking a material for your kitchen counters. Marble looks great in design magazine kitchens, but it may not be the right choice for your family. Here are some tips on the variety of choices available for countertops.

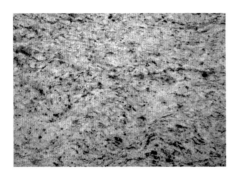

GRANITE—durable, affordable, and available in a variety of colors. I personally love using honed Absolute Black for a soapstonelike effect that is easier to maintain.

CONCRETE—can be formed to the thickness of your liking and stained to a color of your choice. It is incredibly durable and very modern looking.

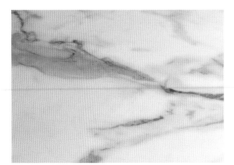

MARBLE—absolutely gorgeous but fickle to live with. It stains and scratches easily, but, boy, does it ever elevate a kitchen to a new level! Sealing is incredibly important with this material, as is careful cleaning.

QUARTZ—a composite, man-made material that is great for busy families with kids due to its stain resistance and tough-as-nails durability. Some brands have patterns that look like natural stone.

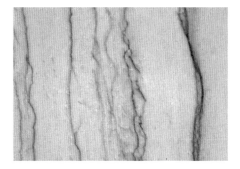

QUARTZITE—I like to think of this as granite masquerading as marble. It has the veiny quality of marble with the durability of granite. A high price comes along with it, however.

BUTCHER BLOCK—looks great on islands and in prep areas. It will need to be oiled and taken care of, but if you are okay with a more rustic patina, it's perfect. It WILL get a bit beat up, but that gives it character.

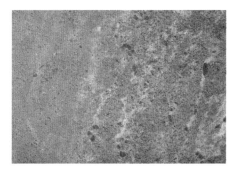

SOAPSTONE—natural and simple but also a tough one with stains. Applying mineral oil helps it resist markings left by water and oily substances.

RIGHT: In this family kitchen we selected a Moroccan-inspired tile for the inlay above the stove to add a pop of color. The pendants and barstools introduce a slightly industrial edge.

OPPOSITE: Eat-in kitchens are so useful for families with children. We defined this area of a city kitchen with bold navy-and-white wallpaper and soft Roman shades. Modern furniture and lighting keeps it clean and unfussy.

THE LIGHTING

LIGHT AND BRIGHT

You want to illuminate every task you do in the kitchen properly—so think long and hard about your lighting plan. Andrew and I stood in our old kitchen for hours discussing exactly where the recessed lighting needed to go. I like to add a dedicated light over the sink as well as under-cabinet lighting to increase flexibility according to need.

A PENCHANT FOR PENDANTS

Pendants act like the jewelry of the kitchen. It took me a long time (and a few visits from the electrician) to decide on the right ones. Small kitchens benefit from clear glass pendants that keep the space feeling open, while large kitchens and kitchen islands can handle larger-scale and more solid fixtures. Make sure they hang higher than your eye level so as not to block your view.

renter's tip

A bad kitchen in a rental can be SO frustrating as major changes just aren't permitted (unless you have deep pockets and a kindly landlord). If you hate your cabinets, try swapping out the hardware for something more your style and paint the walls surrounding them a color you love (if allowed). A great runner or small rug can help conceal an unsightly floor and a few well-selected accents, like a magnificent bowl or bright vase on the counter, can distract the eye.

KITCHEN
ESSENTIALS

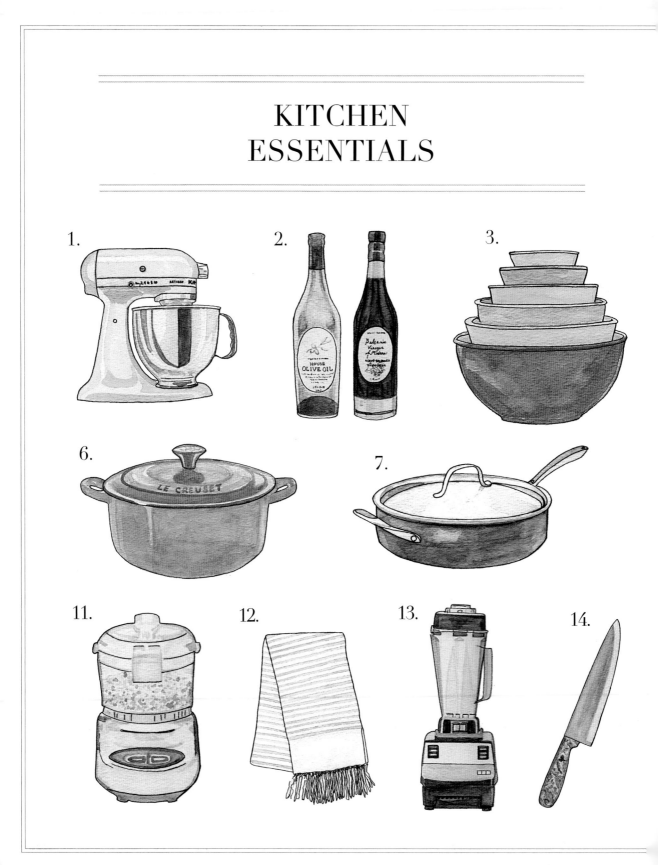

1.

2.

3.

6.

7.

11.

12.

13.

14.

I can't tell you how many times I have found myself rifling through the drawers and cabinets in my kitchen saying things like, "I MUST own a mandoline!" or, "I know I saw a food processor in here once!" We can design the kitchen of our dreams but then fall short when it comes to stocking it with the right tools to make it functional. So I polled some friends and readers who cook a lot more than I do to help me pick out the absolute MUST-haves for any kitchen:

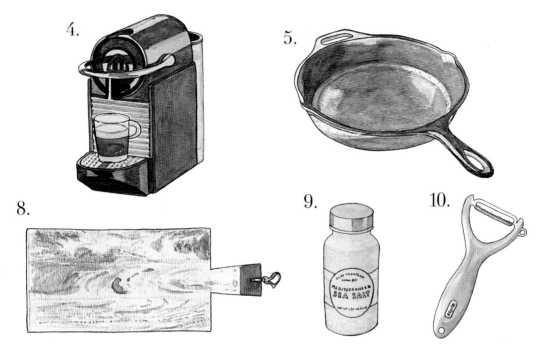

1. Mixer (hand or stand—the latter adds a bit of design bling!)

2. Good olive oil and balsamic vinegar

3. Array of mixing bowls

4. Good coffee machine (I never skimp on this!)

5. A seasoned cast-iron pan (bonus points if you inherit one that's cooked many a meal already!)

6. Dutch oven

7. Big saucepan

8. Good cutting board (pretty enough to serve on too!)

9. Fine sea salt

10. Vegetable peeler

11. Food processor

12. Good, gorgeous dish towels (for décor and sturdy cleanup)

13. High-performance blender

14. Super-sharp chef's knife

TOP 10 RENOVATION LESSONS

LESSON 1: Draw up your ideal budget and then double it and stick a hot poker in your eye. Now you're ready to renovate! People gave me that advice many times before we started and I played Smart Designer Girl and nodded my head but inside thought I had it ALL figured out. I had planned for everything. Except for the stuff I couldn't. Like having to replace corroded pipes in the basement. All of them. And wires. All of them. Until you open up your walls, all those numbers might as well be written in invisible ink or crayon. Plan accordingly.

LESSON 2: Everything that gets added on is at least $250. Everything. There is nothing in the world that costs less than that. Wire for sconces? $250. Patch a wall? $250. Punch yourself in the face? $250. CASH. I got to the point where it all felt like Monopoly money. I'd get a call: "So, we kind of need to reframe that doorway . . ." And I'd be like, "Add it to my tab!" Every. Single. Time. Until you GET your tab and then pass out because you think you'll have to start working the night shift at Mickey D's to pay for it all.

LESSON 3: Pay attention. To everything. I am a professional in the field and even I messed this one up. None of the people you hire can read your mind or know the gray grout that was delivered is one shade too light. Even when you have someone reputable managing your project, you have to pay attention to all the details. This stands true for money and invoices, products being used, finish work being done (what "ceiling white" means to one person does not always mean the same to another) and time frame expectations. You are the boss of this project and need to act like one.

LESSON 4: This isn't personal, it's business. It's very *Godfather*-esque but you need to keep that in mind. This holds especially true for women managing their own renovations—we can err on the side of doormat in order to not be seen as a bitch. Well,

OPPOSITE: We added some personality to this contractor-designed kitchen with a pair of industrial metal islands, a graphic Madeline Weinrib rug, and some modern pendants.

time to scrap that worry, because this is your money being spent and you need to stand up for it (and yourself). If something isn't up to snuff, even if it seems picky—ask for it to be redone. If something is taking too long, bring it up! This is not the time and place to worry about being seen as difficult or demanding. Be sure to deliver all questions, demands, and the like with a calm tone of voice but with conviction.

LESSON 5: Make the basics CLASSIC. By classic, I don't mean everything has to be traditional, but stick to clean lines and neutral colors when it comes to cabinets, counters, and appliances. It's much easier (and cheaper) to rip out and replace a backsplash or swap hardware than cabinets! Even if you don't plan on reselling your house anytime soon, your future self (with different taste) will thank you.

LESSON 6: You CAN mix metals. I did it; so can you. Not everything in the kitchen has to be all chrome or nickel or brass, even! Mixing metals can punch up the personality of your space—but please stick to only two. Having five different metal finishes looks schizophrenic, not eclectic.

LESSON 7: When planning your cabinets, think about what's going in them. Too many times people have designed a kitchen around look and not function. This has to be THE most functional room in your home. While beauty is always a focus, so is where you plan to store your Tupperware. Lay out the kitchen and then notate on the plans exactly what is going in each cabinet or drawer. It may make you realize you need more space in one area or less in another. Or maybe you don't want to put that Tupperware in a glass-front cabinet.

LESSON 8: More expensive appliances can make a budget-friendly kitchen look like it costs more than it did—and can make prospective buyers assume the entire house is also expensively furnished. My dad told me once that when buyers see a fancy range, they then assume the bathrooms are all at that level too. Spend where it counts, and save where it doesn't. Expensive white subway tile is hard to discern from cheap subway . . . but everyone will notice a subpar stove.

LESSON 9: Gather inspiration, but then be realistic about the space you actually have to work with. A huge island with pendants may be on your dream kitchen list,

but if the shape of your room isn't conducive to it, then you need to think about how you can work in that look but in a different way. Don't try to make your kitchen something it's not going to be. Be honest to your vision but also with yourself about what's possible.

LESSON 10: Listen to your spouse and family members about what they envision too. This is the space in the home most used by everyone. If your significant other MUST have a pull-down spray faucet, by all means consider it. It might mean they'll do more dishes and that you can then get your marble counters (which are a pain to keep stain free, by the way!)

LASTLY, THIS IS NOT THE END OF THE WORLD. Although it might feel like that sometimes—I know I felt that way—but know that this is the best place to spend money in your house. You will not only enjoy it for years to come, but when you sell your home, you will also get more of your investment in this room back than any other in a house.

OH AND LESSON 11 . . . HAVE LOTS AND LOTS OF WINE ON HAND. LOTS. CHEERS.

MY BEST
BALSAMIC DRESSING

I always make my own salad dressing, even when I'm dining alone. It's so much better than any bottled version, and now my family always puts me on dressing duty for the holidays. I guess they like it.

2 tablespoons good balsamic vinegar

1 tablespoon extra virgin olive oil

1 tablespoon Dijon mustard

1 tablespoon maple syrup

Squeeze of fresh lemon juice

Salt and pepper to taste

Whisk together and toss into any salad. Also good simple with baby spinach!

RIGHT: A gleaming New York kitchen done in all white and marble. We added softness with sheer linen window treatments and linen-upholstered barstools at the counter.

GRANDMA GATES'S CONGO BARS

Andrew's maternal grandparents were a couple of the coolest people I've ever met. While I did not get to know his grandmother well due to her dementia, I do know a lot about her from all the wonderful stories her family tells about her love for crafts (especially those involving moss, fungus, and wreaths), swimming, and her congo bars she made for all her grandkids.

⅔ cup butter

1 pound brown sugar

3 eggs

2⅔ cups sifted flour

½ teaspoon salt

2½ teaspoons baking powder

1 cup chopped pecans

8 ounces chocolate chips

1 teaspoon vanilla

Melt butter in large saucepan. Stir in the brown sugar and heat until the sugar dissolves. Remove saucepan from heat and add eggs one at a time, beating well. In a separate bowl, combine flour, salt, and baking powder. Stir the dry ingredients into the butter-sugar mixture a third at a time. Fold in pecans and chocolate chips. Stir in the vanilla. Spread in a greased 10 x 14-inch pan. Bake at 350 for 25–30 minutes, making sure not to overcook. Cut into squares.

MOM'S FAMOUS MARINADE

My grandmother gave this recipe to my mother, who then gave it to me. It works best on steak, but is great for fish like swordfish as well. Cut this in half unless you are entertaining.

1½ cups canola oil

¾ cup soy sauce

¼ cup Worcestershire sauce

2 tablespoons dry mustard

1 tablespoon coarse black pepper

½ cup red wine vinegar

1½ teaspoons parsley

⅓ cup lemon juice

Garlic as desired

Marinate overnight in a Tupperware container for best taste.

OPPOSITE, TOP TO BOTTOM: Lining the interior of glass cabinetry with wallpaper is a great way to add interest. The large waterfall island provides ample prep space as well as a dining area. Glass pendants and acrylic barstools keep it from feeling too crowded. • This client's gorgeous sink made of honed black granite provides a seamless, rustic look to her kitchen.

ABOVE: No cabinets for all your glasses? A free-standing piece can work wonders, especially if you paint the interior a color!

ANDREW'S FAVORITE BEEF STEW

This super-easy-to-make recipe is proof positive that the way to a man's heart is through his stomach. When this is cooking in the slow cooker, Andrew is madly in love with me. My mom made this for us growing up and to me, love smells like beef stew.

- 1 pound stew beef, cut into 1–2-inch cubes
- 1 tablespoon olive oil
- 1–2 cups each of cubed potatoes, baby carrots, chopped celery, peas, chopped onions, whatever you like!
- 1 packet of McCormick Bag 'N Season or Beef Stew spice mix
- 1 six-ounce can tomato sauce (not pasta sauce!)
- 6 ounces red wine (plus some to sip)

Brown the beef in the olive oil. Put into a big, heavy Dutch oven (like Le Creuset's) along with all your veggies. Stir in the seasoning packet and water as instructed on back of packet and add the can of tomato sauce. Refill empty sauce can with red wine and stir together. Cook at 350 degrees for 2½–3 hours. Alternatively, you can cook in a Crock-Pot on low for 6–8 hours (the house will smell amazing when you come home!).

THE DINING
ROOM

DOWN THE AISLE IN STYLE (AND SMOKE)

Those of us who struggle with perfectionism make both the best and worst entertainers. Our inner Martha Stewart wants to impress on all fronts, whipping up a Cornish game hen with stuffing made from homemade croutons while simultaneously arranging a preserved lemon-and-orchid centerpiece AND baking a cheesecake in a drop-dead outfit to the tunes of our perfectly assembled playlists. But the stress of it all can leave us a flour-covered, weepy mess. When Pinterest-perfect images are assaulting us from all sides, it's hard not to feel inadequate when planning a dinner for friends and family.

I love the concept of entertaining, but I can easily get overwhelmed, the joy of it all evaporating as swiftly as I can burn a

---

OPPOSITE: Our dining room may be small, but we've made some big statements in it. The Sputnik-inspired light fixture in brass is a modern throwback that was a hard-fought battle to get approved by my husband!

batch of cookies. I'm not the most skilled cook either. I can't even handle raw chicken without gagging, never mind defeathering a turkey raised organically on my own farm. And I certainly can't do it while being a charming and pleasant hostess. So I've adapted my entertaining style to suit my skills, but only after learning some really good lessons from throwing the biggest dinner party ever—my own wedding.

When I began planning my wedding, I was incredibly naïve and delirious about the whole thing. Knowing my parents' nervous systems couldn't handle hosting 145 people at their beautiful house, we decided to have the wedding at a gorgeous old manor nearby. It was the stuff dreams and Ralph Lauren ads are made of—fireplaces, dark wood molding and gilt-framed paintings, a romantic garden with stone walls, and candlelight everywhere. Being an aesthetically minded person, I figured that putting together this party to end all parties in a setting as gorgeous as this one would be a relative breeze. And I had a bevy of bridesmaids at the ready to help me with whatever details I needed (not that I would let anyone help, as I am a certifiable control freak). I was supremely confident it was going to be a flawless experience.

My first clue that it wasn't going to go that way should have been my dress. This is the most important single garment I would ever wear in my life, and the knowledge it was supposed to make a statement that defined my whole betrothal freaked me out. Was I a modern bride? A classic bride? A froufrou bride? A sexy bride? After trying on several dresses that easily could have been "the one," I snubbed them all and insisted on going to a fancy designer's boutique because I had my heart set on wearing her very specific label.

Mistake number one. I was mismeasured by the staff and when my dress came in six months later, it didn't even come close to fitting. And they weren't able to fix it without it costing thousands more. They had made me sign a document when I ordered it that I had to pay for the dress anyway. Post-fitting, I stumbled onto the street in hysterics, dissolving into a puddle of regret and anger and sobbing on the pavement. I had to find a new dress in three months and it had to be a bargain, because I (and by "I," I actually mean my dad) was thousands of dollars in the red. Not the best way to start off the happiest day of your life.

But while I was busy dealing with that catastrophe, I had to think about flowers, invitations, seating charts, vows, and menus. Thank goodness the venue we picked was run like a machine (a James Beard Award–winning machine) and those decisions came together quite easily. This was the pre-Pinterest/wedding blog era, so I always came to each vendor meeting armed with tear sheets and pictures of the

The gray grass cloth in our dining room is my most favorite thing in the entire house. I love the depth it creates in this small space. A close second—our amazing light fixture!

before

things I wanted. I was painfully specific and confident, so how could anything go wrong?

Well, as with most events, a lot did. Starting with the weather. We were married September 17, 2005, and we had picked the date thinking it would be a mild day in the '60s, as New England Septembers are wont to be. Not that year, though. I woke up to a hot, hazy, and humid 92-degree day with the threat of storms. Getting zipped into my heavy satin dress (which I hated), I already felt beads of sweat rolling down my back. With paper towels stuffed under my armpits to soak up the sweat, I raced around the house trying to deal with a missing shipment of miniature pears that would hold the place cards (complete with vintage pins). Meanwhile, my brother was on his way to the hospital because he had just stabbed himself in the leg with a box cutter trying to cut cardboard to make a special container to house his wedding gift. This was more than good ol' Lady Speedstick could handle.

But I pulled it together for the pictures (my brother missed a few while getting stitches), dabbing my brow with tissue between takes and cursing my decision to wear Spanx. As my maids and I piled into the limo, I breathed a sigh of relief as the air-conditioning cooled me down and the drive to the mansion began.

BUT I HAD RELAXED TOO SOON.

Not long into our drive I thought I noticed the inside of the limo getting smoky. I asked anyone else if they noticed it or maybe my Spanx were just too tight and my vision had become compromised. But the girls agreed, and as we rolled down the partition to speak to the driver about it, I noticed the blare of sirens and flashing red-and-blue lights behind us. We were being pulled over by a cop. But the driver wasn't slowing down.

"Um, sir?" I said. "I think you need to pull over for that cop."

"I can't," he calmly replied. "Our brakes have gone out."

It took a second for me to register this new information. I really, really didn't want to die on my wedding day. It would really cast a pall over the event we'd spent so much money on. Thank goodness for my calm bridesmaids who talked me off the ledge as the driver pulled the emergency brake and the limo slowly rolled to a stop on the side of the highway. As we all calmed down a bit, I recalled that Andrew's first wife's limo had also broken down on the way to their wedding and they'd gotten separated ninety days later! I looked at my soon-to-be sister-in-law and could tell she knew exactly what I was thinking. She just said, "No, don't even think about that. This is not a sign!" Still, the coincidence was uncanny . . . and unnerving to a bride about to walk down the aisle.

Fully expecting the cop to be valiant and helpful to our stranded bridal party, I was floored when he came up to the car and demanded we all get out of the limo while he searched the vehicle.

"Um, sir, please. It's my wedding day. I assure you we are not smuggling any drugs in all this satin!"

"Please just exit the vehicle, ma'am."

"ARE YOU SERIOUS? You want me to get out onto the highway in my wedding dress?"

"Yes, ma'am."

And that's how I ended up standing on the side of a three-lane highway in front of a McDonald's in my wedding gown. As I wondered what to do (and considered getting a cheeseburger), I saw my soon-to-be brother-in-law driving by in his car wearing a look of complete confusion and bewilderment on his face. He pulled over with a screech and manipulated all seven of our finely attired butts into his Ford Explorer.

Cursing and laughing, we arrived at the manor like clowns in a car, me unfolding myself out of the front seat in front of waiting guests as my parents hurried over to make sure I wasn't going to need to be medicated and put in a padded room. Somehow I made it down the aisle to my waiting groom and said "I do" under a canopy of flowers, nearly on time. As we clinked our glasses for our first toast, the thunder rolled in, the rain began coming down, but all I could do was laugh.

It was far from perfect—hot as hell inside, people drenched in sweat, a bar bill triple what was estimated, and a glass of red wine spilled down the back of my dress halfway through the reception—but, man, was it fun. Everyone was glowing with happiness on the dance floor as our awesome band played our favorite tunes and all the people we loved surrounded us and helped make our marriage official.

WHEN IT COMES DOWN TO IT, THROWING A GOOD PARTY HAS MANY PARTS, BUT IT'S ALL ABOUT THE PEOPLE YOU CARE FOR GATHERING TOGETHER.

When it comes down to it, throwing a good party has many parts, but it's all about the people you care for gathering together. You could serve pizza and wine, and I guarantee you your guests will have just as much fun as if you had put out calligraphic place cards and a chocolate soufflé. Every time I hear someone say, "That was one awesome party" about our wedding, I'm reminded of all the good things—not the heat, the cops, the rain, or the last-minute dress, but the happy faces of my family and friends. Just another example of how entertaining is all about love, laughs, and a boatload of mistakes.

DEFINE YOUR STYLE: DINING ROOM

modern

Raw edge table, cantilever seating, bold lighting, and graphic drapes.

eclectic

Contemporary marble, Louis chairs, brass fixtures, and ikat drapes.

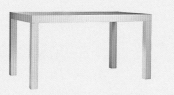 

glamorous

Parsons table, lacquer chairs, blingy light, and graphic wallpaper.

traditional

Pedestal table, tufted chairs, vintage chandelier, and paisley drapes.

new country

Rustic table, slipcovered seating, overscale lantern, and grass-cloth walls.

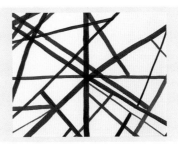

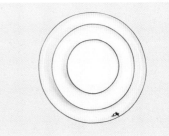

OPPOSITE: An informal dining area off our client's kitchen gets a country makeover thanks to bentwood chairs, turned-leg table, and slipcovered end chairs.

LEFT: The table set for dinner.

SETTING THE TABLE

I remember after I got engaged, I skipped through store aisles with a scanner gun as I filled up my registry with all sorts of tabletop goodies. And when it came to one of the most important registry items, my china pattern, I went with simple and plain over patterned and historical. I have to say it's a big regret of mine. To be honest, I think I've used my china a total of five times in eight years—partially because we don't formally entertain that often but also because it bores me to death. Why didn't I get something magical and bold from Bernardaud? Or a classic from Herend? I was scared, plain and simple, of making the wrong choice. But I have learned that when setting a table, it's all about the mix! One set of china, no matter how graphic and colorful, is uninteresting on its own, just like a matching bedroom set (word to the wise, never buy a set of anything that is furniture related. EVER). Here are a few tips to help you set a creative and gorgeous table.

CHARGERS AND SALAD PLATES
TO THE RESCUE!

No matter how basic your china is, adding different chargers and salad plates really makes it look unique. I love using patterned salad or dessert plates in combination with my classic china and a metallic charger—and it's not expensive to do. Try searching your local discount store for options!

FLASHY FLATWARE

From gold to matte black, from twig-shaped handles to bamboo accents, there are tons of choices out there these days for interesting flatware to excite dining companions. Consider investing in a fun set of flatware to use with your plain china or to dress up a setting of your everyday dishes!

GORGEOUS GLASSWARE

One of my favorite possessions is my set of turquoise-blue French opaline wineglasses. I picked them up at an antiques show and I can't tell you how many compliments I get on them when I set them out for dinners! Mixing colored water glasses or wineglasses with a clear, basic set adds color and texture to an otherwise monochromatic table.

OPPOSITE, LEFT TO RIGHT: Pretty, classic, pewter-rimmed plates are topped off with patterned napkins and paired with green glassware playing off the dining-room color scheme. Fun bamboo flatware adds a more casual flair and the white blossoms of various flowers add texture. • Mixing gold and silver china is possible with the right accent plate! Adding a textured charger and tassel napkin ring ratchets up the glam factor.

ABOVE, LEFT TO RIGHT: A rather traditional china pattern is combined with modern dip-dye napkins and gold flatware, creating a fun and funky mix. One of my favorite looks! • Modern and graphic napkins funkify delicate, traditional china.

ABOVE: The bold green distressed finish on the chest, which serves as a buffet, plays gorgeously off the abstract work by Mallory Page. Blue-and-white ginger jars add a classic touch.

OPPOSITE: In this Beacon Hill town house, the dining room combines historical details with modern touches. The walls are painted in Farrow & Ball Cornforth White.

OPPOSITE: A photograph taken by the homeowner was blown up to a large scale. Paired with the beachy faux bamboo chairs and rustic wood table, it creates a soothing place to chow down.

LEFT: A beachy table setting with raffia placemats, blue-and-white china, and a long-lasting succulent centerpiece.

LINENS AND THINGS

Having an array of linen options available to use is key when setting a table—from various colors and patterns to luxurious monograms. Sometimes keeping everything else simple and using a bright solid napkin or a funky black-and-white stripe is all you need to take your table from boring to beautiful.

FRONT AND CENTER

Creating a centerpiece can be daunting. Try not to go too crazy and stick to these quick and easy tips:

- BUY A COUPLE VARIETIES OF FLOWERS, but all in the same color, and put them in vases of varying heights clustered in the center or down the length of a table.

- FIND A GREAT TRAY and top it with white pillar candles of varying heights for a nonfloral option.

- FILL A BIG BOWL (or several bowls on a rectangular table) with preserved green moss.

- AVOID ANYTHING TOO TALL that keeps people from being able to look each other in the eye or pass food.

- DON'T GO OVERBOARD so that you can't fit serving platters on the table too!

renter's tip

Some rentals come prelit with hideous dining room fixtures. Instead of accepting this as something you can't change and cursing the offending light every time you enter the room, consider spending the money to have a licensed electrician swap in one of your choice. As long as you store the existing fixture and reinstall it before you move out, your security deposit will be safe.

ABOVE: This client's red-lacquer dining table is statement enough, but paired with red ikat bowls and pink flowers, it's even more fun.

OPPOSITE: In a cute little condo dining area, we paired an antique-looking chandelier with another tulip table (we love them; can you tell?). A map of Nantucket was blown up and split into a grid of frames, an affordable option for large wall art.

OPPOSITE: Another example of mixing modern and traditional in this Boston dining room. The neon sign above the mantel was an amazing find by the client.

ABOVE: Our crafty client had small logs cut down and applied to the nonworking face of the old fireplace. Such a great way to dress up a nonfunctioning hearth!

HOW TO PICK A PERFECT PAINT COLOR

The most asked questions I get in my business are about paint color. This seems to be an area in which people feel an intense amount of distrust in their vision and ability to choose. Color is a personal choice that can be polarizing for a lot of people, so be true to yourself and use colors you find yourself extremely attracted to.

SWATCH WATCH

Looking at paint swatches can be seriously overwhelming. There are SO many options out there for every color under the sun. Once you've decided on the color you want for the room, look for a color you are instantly drawn to and then consider one a shade or even two lighter and one a shade darker. Color looks very different on a small scale than it does on four big walls! Grays can look blue, and pinks and yellows are always MUCH more vibrant than the sample appears. The key is testing.

OPPOSITE: Before we started this project, the dining room was bright red and super traditional. After we got our hands on it, it has a much more modern feel thanks to its new gray hue (Benjamin Moore Dolphin). The client and I drove hours through nowhere Pennsylvania to pick out the slab for this custom table.

TESTING, TESTING

I always advise clients to buy sample pots of actual paint instead of picking from swatches alone (most swatches aren't samples of the actual paint, after all). Apply a two-coat, 12-inch-square sample on at least two walls in the space you are painting, as each wall will get different light. Observe them in daylight, twilight, and evening light to see if the subtle color changes are ones you can live with.

ABOVE, LEFT TO RIGHT: This area is narrow, so we had a custom-designed slim china cabinet and plate rack installed to store formal tableware and wineglasses. • Banquette detail—Schumacher's Chiang Mai Dragon and silver nailheads.

OPPOSITE: A custom banquette in a bold fabric is a true standout in this space. Paired with modern classics and set in front of a rich blue wall (Benjamin Moore Summer Nights), this open dining space feels surprisingly cozy.

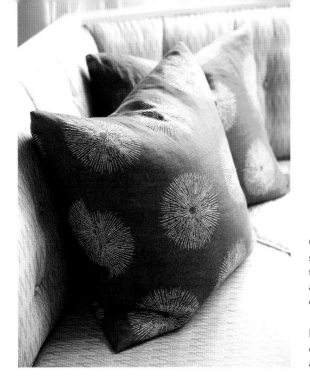

OPPOSITE: A casual nook designed especially for family dinners, this custom banquette and table create the perfect spot for a quick snack or longer dinner.

LEFT: Adding throw pillows to a dining banquette injects comfort and color.

FINISH IT OFF

The finish of paint you need depends on the space you're painting. Here's a quick guide to help you decide:

MATTE/FLAT: Good for ceilings and rooms that don't get a lot of traffic, as it is hard to clean.

EGGSHELL: The most popular finish for living area walls (living rooms, dining rooms, bedrooms, offices). Easier to clean.

SATIN: Use for high traffic or damp areas that are cleaned often, such as bathrooms, kitchens, and children's spaces. A low-shine finish is a good choice for woodwork.

SEMIGLOSS: This is a great choice for kitchens and bathrooms due to its ability to resist humidity well. However, it does have a sheen to it. I use semigloss mostly on trim and woodwork.

HIGH GLOSS: A dramatic choice that only works if the surface you are painting is very smooth, as it reflects imperfections. Great for dramatic dark colors or woodwork.

ABOVE, LEFT TO RIGHT: An old hand-me-down dining chair from Andrew's grandparents was revived with a coat of high gloss paint and new zebra upholstery. Never overlook well-made family heirlooms. • A crisp and modern dining area pairs a marble tulip table with Louis Ghost chairs and a super-modern light fixture.

OPPOSITE: Louis-style dining chairs upholstered in brown velvet create a vintage look while the custom drapes cuffed in green velvet add a luxe touch.

MY FORTY-FIVE FAVORITE PAINT COLORS

I've been asked time and time again what my favorite paint colors
are, so here is a selection of the best hues under the rainbow
for you to try in your own home.

FB Pale Hound · FB Dayroom Yellow · S-W Sagey · FB Green Ground · B Sliced Cucumber

BM Wedgewood Gray · FB Stone Blue · PL Delft Blue · FB Hague Blue · PL Divinity

BM Manchester Tan · FB Skimming Stone · FB Cornforth White · BM Silver Satin · FB Elephant's Breath

BM Stonington Gray · BM Balboa Mist · S-W Repose Gray · PL Winter's Gate · B Elephant Skin

B: BEHR • BM: BENJAMIN MOORE • FB: FARROW & BALL

PL Red Banner   V Creme Caramel   BM All-A-Blaze   S-W Diminutive Pink   BM Blanched Coral

BM Palladian Blue   FB Arsenic   FB Green Smoke   BM Deep River   BM Glass Slipper

FB Calluna   B French Lilac   FB Pelt   BM Edgecomb Gray   BM Athena

BM Bleecker Beige   B Anonymous   FB Mahogany   BM Shoreline   PL Mirage Grey

PL Ever Classic   BM Chelsea Gray   BM Kendall Charcoal   FB Down Pipe   FB Pitch Black

PL: PRATT & LAMBERT   •   S-W: SHERWIN-WILLIAMS   •   V: VALSPAR

THE FAMILY ROOM

LIQUID, CHICKEN-FLAVORED XANAX

W hile I don't have any children yet, or a separate space to dedicate as a family room, that doesn't mean I don't have a family. I do. Just half of the members have four legs and fur. If you know me at all, you know I worship my dogs. It's a sickness I like to blame on my parents because they never got me a dog as a child. Granted I had cats, all sorts of cats taken in off the street and such, and one very important "cat-dog" named Tigger (who acted more like a dog than a cat by doing things like waiting for my school bus at the end of the driveway). Tigger died at the age of twenty-one (I'm not exaggerating even a little) and after that we became a dog family.

OPPOSITE: Deep-purple custom pillows on a family room sofa.

My mom rescued our first dog from certain death at a puppy shop in the mall. She was driving forty-five minutes there every day and instead of having a shopping addiction, as my dad suspected, she was actually going to look at this sad little mutt in a cage. Something in his monkeylike eyes had ensnared my mom's heart. She feared that Y2K was going to happen and the world was going to explode from a rogue rounding error and this pup would never know love. So she petitioned my dad to go look at him. Expecting some sort of retriever or hound or some recognizable form of the canine family, he was instead introduced to a thin-haired rodent-mutt. Taking in the dog's spotted skin, scrawny legs, and tufts of white hair, my dad didn't even know what to say to my mom other than, "Are you sure you're feeling okay?" But they came home with him (for $150, including a crate, food, toys, and collar), and gosh-darn-it, the Tubridy family had a dog named Tucker. He and I bonded from the get-go. He was so sweet and thankful to be spared from being euthanized that he just made everyone fall in love with him. His hair grew in and he filled out and became a cutie-pie—a schnoodle, we found out—and turned me into a dog person.

I was scared shitless of dogs as a kid. Our neighbor had this devil spawn named Dancer, a Doberman pinscher I was sure had a taste for blood. Especially the blood of unibrowed, elementary school girls. The dog was not allowed inside and was instead kept in a pen in their backyard. At the time I didn't think of this as cruel, but it was, and so it was no surprise that Dancer liked to escape this pen and run around our yard and scare us half to death. To an eight-year-old he resembled more of a velociraptor than a dog. I recall one afternoon when that furry spawn of Satan got out and disturbed an otherwise fabulous game of fort my brother Mike and I were playing. We huddled in the bushes trying not to cry audibly as Dancer ran circles around the house. We tried to time our sprint for the door as Dancer lapped the house again and again. In a classic anxiety-stricken moment I began worrying about the door being locked. I don't think it ever was locked in all of my childhood but with my luck this ONE TIME it would be and I would become a little Doberman snack cake. This is why I really dug cats for a very long time.

But as an adult I could not WAIT to get a dog. After Andrew and I got married and moved into a condo with a small yard, I began my search for the perfect dog. I read all about various breeds, temperaments, and grooming schedules and decided on a breed the *New York Times* had dubbed "hot": the Havanese. Tiny, smart, nonshedding, and cute as hell, this was all I wanted in a dog. I found a breeder in Connecticut and put my name on a waitlist for the next litter. I didn't even care about the exorbitant price of what was to be a twelve-pound dog—I simply obsessed over Havanese puppy pictures online for months until I got the call that the litter had been born. I was a mommy!

I knew I wanted a boy because I prefer boys in every which way. Being the only girl with three brothers and knowing what a pain in the ass I was/am, I always seem to prefer boys. My mom and I went to the breeder to pick up my puppy and came face-to-face with a box of wriggling black hamsterlike creatures. They were merely a few weeks old and I could hardly tell which one would be the most fun, mentally stable, and adorable of all of them. So I picked the only one with a cute little white chin and chest and named him Baxter. We had to wait over a month until we could take him home and I prepared for his arrival with toys, treats, bowls, beds, and, to Andrew's chagrin, little puppy sweaters. I was going to be the most prepared dog mom in HISTORY and Baxter was going to be the perfect little best friend.

Our first months with little Baxter were bliss—he was hysterically dopey and silly, sweet, and oh so cute. He learned tricks and cuddled and wrestled with his dad and his dog aunts and uncles. And then he slowly began to develop an anxiety disorder. Any loud noise gave him a mean case of the shakes. So did rain. Or snow. He didn't want to go for walks with me and preferred the comfort of his little

nest under the bed. And things only got worse over time. Cut to present day, when I spend $25 every few months to fill his prescription for liquid, chicken-flavored Xanax. REAL, human-grade Xanax. And it's specially blended into a liquid, chicken-flavored form because he is so super-DUPER crazy that he won't take pills. I have to pry his jaws open and squirt in his dose quickly to avoid getting mauled. Sometimes I think perhaps the breeder mated his mother with an anxiety-riddled great white shark. I could hide a teeny-tiny pill in a turkey carcass chock-full of delicious white meat and that dog would run under the sofa and stay there for DAYS. And speaking of turkey, he's the only dog I have ever met who actually

ABOVE: I may not have children or a separate family room, but living with these two monsters has its own challenges.

doesn't like to eat. He turns his nose up at everything I serve him, apparently in an attempt to maintain his supermodel-like lithe figure. I guess Forrest Gump was right, you never know what you're gonna get!

Since then we have also recued a pup named Oliver, some kind of Havanese-Bichon-Poodle blend of pure awesome. He's the opposite of Baxter, a totally laidback dude, loves food more than anything, and is just pure positive energy. And while these two could not be more opposite, they happen to be best friends. It made me realize just how much opposites attract, just like my Andrew and me. Baxter and I are alike

in our raging anxiety and prescription drugs while Andrew and Oliver are naturally happy and relaxed. Parenting them, if you could call it that, has taught us a lot about patience, understanding, and, for me in particular, letting go of my vise grip on perfection.

Like kids, living with pets is a messy business. They drag mud into the house, chew stuff, shed, leave toys everywhere (I swear the dog toys procreate while I'm sleeping), and even occasionally pee on things. They see nothing wrong with rolling in a pile of mulch and then running up to your bedroom to shake it off on your nice white duvet cover. I almost had an

absolute coronary the day after our new linen sofa arrived when my two furry idiots jumped on it with mud on their paws. After a while you learn that messes are part of life, and well worth it in exchange for all the love your pets (or kids) give you. You have to adapt the way you live and your interior spaces to work with them instead of against them. No, your family room will probably never look good enough to have Kate Middleton over for a play date, but that's okay. And if one of my dogs barfs on the guestroom rug, it's not the end of the world. It's real life. And sometimes that life just needs to be sprayed top to bottom with Scotchgard.

OPPOSITE, LEFT TO RIGHT: The bright art inspired the palette for the room. • A cozy window seat combining ikat-print pillows and a small-scale geometric fabric cushion.

ABOVE, LEFT TO RIGHT: Children's toys need not be detrimental to your décor. This white play kitchen and miniature-scale modern chair fit right in with the grown-up furniture! • This large family room has space for everything—books, toys, and lots of spots to curl up and watch a movie. The gray-and-purple palette is carried through from other rooms in the home. The walls here are painted in Farrow & Ball Plummett.

OPPOSITE: A blend of traditional and modern pieces make for an interesting and personal space.

LEFT: Brass library sconces and a sunburst mirror act as stylish accents above the fireplace.

FIXING UP THE FAMILY ROOM

Family rooms are probably one of the most used and multipurpose rooms in a house. If you're lucky enough to have a separate space like this, it typically has to serve as a place to corral kids and toys, watch TV, work, and entertain. But that doesn't mean it can't look good while doing all that. Keeping things simple, sturdy, and streamlined is the name of the game in this type of room.

We painted all the woodwork in this family den a deep gray (Farrow & Ball Downpipe) and covered the walls in a warm grass cloth to create a truly enveloping feeling.

A SPECTACULAR SECTIONAL

No, it's not an oxymoron; there ARE great-looking sectionals that can withstand your family fun time and still be acceptable to guests. Look for ones that have sturdy pillows and cushions and simple, classic lines. Tight-back sectionals, like mine, look neat and tidy most of the time (and prevent pets from sleeping on the back pillows and crushing them to a point where they can no longer be fluffed up!). Upholstery in a dark color or an indoor/outdoor fabric is also helpful when it comes to stains and the rogue marker!

ABOVE: Turquoise grass cloth behind a set of built-ins show off a collection of accessories.

OPPOSITE: A large living space flows right into the family/dining area and kitchen, allowing for a casual, open lifestyle.

TOUGH-WEARING SOFT GOODS

We always advise our clients to consider indoor/outdoor upholstery fabric and rugs for family room use. There are such wonderful-looking (and feeling) outdoor fabrics on the market, so you won't be compromising on style at all. And being able to hose off a rug covered in chocolate milk is something you might thank me for someday!

OPPOSITE: We advised a somewhat color-shy client to add small pops of navy and cobalt to the scheme of this welcoming family den, creating an inviting and happy blend of tones.

ABOVE: Yellow and blue patterns make a bright and cheerful space for the whole family.

STORAGE, STORAGE, STORAGE

The key to a great family room is buying and installing the best and most attractive storage system you can afford—be it built-in bookshelves and cabinets or freestanding shelving with bins and baskets. And remember, they don't all have to be kid-themed pieces—simple white Parsons-style bookcases with woven baskets look chic and grown-up while concealing the seven thousand Legos the kids have.

OPPOSITE, TOP TO BOTTOM: Creating a dedicated casual living space in a large open room is possible, as we did with this custom-designed sectional and ottoman. • A vivid mix of colors and patterns.

ABOVE: A large-scale photograph of the Hamptons, where this client has a summer home, reminds the family daily of their favorite place to vacation.

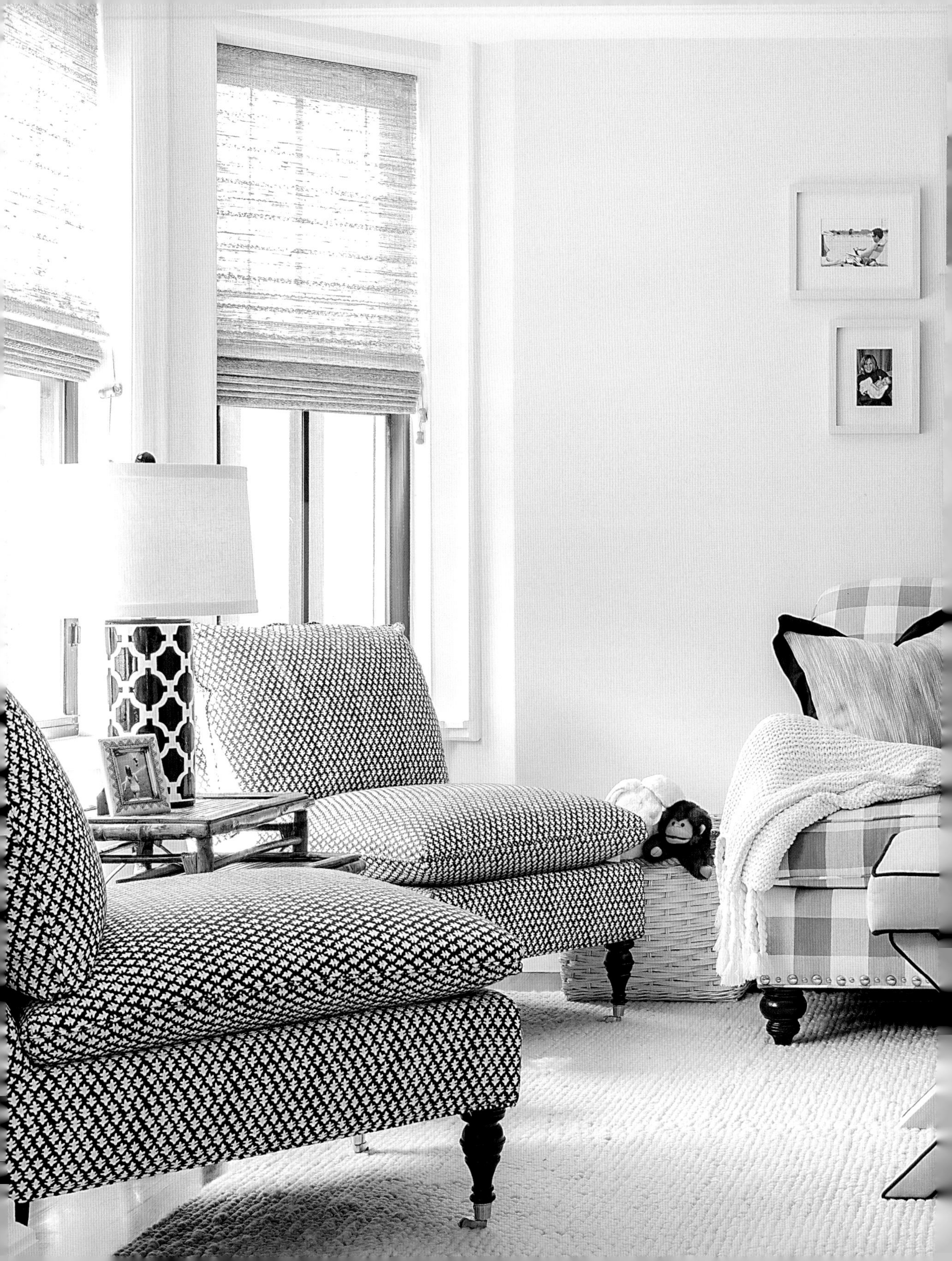

We loved pulling together all these colors and patterns in this city family room—a pair of navy-piped violet x-benches easily moves out of the way for more floor space for the babies to play!

DEALING WITH THE TV

Whether it's in your living room or in the family room (or both), dealing with the TV can be tricky. Of course, these days they seem to be getting bigger and bigger (yet thinner) so finding a way to watch your favorite shows while not letting the TV overpower the room can be a puzzle to solve. Good thing there are so many amazing options for housing, mounting, and concealing TVs. Here are a few examples of how we've worked them into the décor.

ABOVE, LEFT TO RIGHT: We designed a custom built-in with doors in a recessed area of this living room to house the TV and allow for it to be easily concealed. • Papering the walls behind the TV and bookshelves in this built-in are an unapologetic way of drawing the eye instead of ushering it past.

GOOD TO GREAT

As new houses get bigger and bigger, great rooms have replaced separate dedicated family rooms. A giant room is great for families who need space to spread out and play, but designing one can leave you stumped as to how to make it feel less cavernous. Try laying the room out with a couple of separate seating areas—maybe one for TV viewing, with two large sofas, and another for reading, consisting of four comfy chairs facing one another. A small casual table in a corner can serve as a place to sit down for a snack or play a game. Make sure your furniture reflects the scale of the room—lots of teeny-tiny furniture will make the room feel busy.

ABOVE, LEFT TO RIGHT: Real people have real stuff, and finding a way to store and display it in a pleasing way is key. This space is another example of decorating around the TV instead of trying to hide it. • I had no choice but to mount my own TV above the fireplace, a typical decorating no-no. By adding cool accessories, I tried to make it as pleasing to the eye as possible.

HOW TO HANG ART

Some quick and easy examples of ways to display art in your home, one of the MOST important accents you can add to a space!

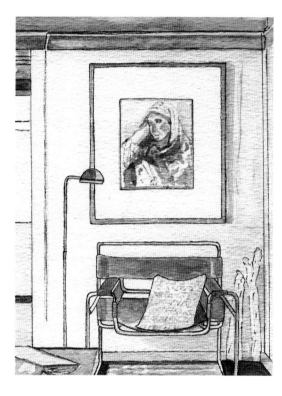

THE STATEMENT

One large work of art above a sofa or substantial piece of furniture really anchors a room and makes a lasting impression. Whether a photograph, painting, or drawing, make sure it is proportionally significant in relation to whatever it is hanging above or the wall it's on. If it's too small, it will look lost. Go big or go home here; otherwise, consider multiple pieces.

THE LEANER

To give a larger grouping of art a more casual look, consider installing simple floating shelves and leaning the pieces against the wall, layered over one another. Frames of the same finish will keep your arrangement from looking too messy and haphazard. You can also create a version of this style atop a long console or buffet table.

GALLERY WALL

One of our most requested services is hanging art on gallery walls. My secret to creating a haphazard grouping is to simply wing it! Too much exact measuring will leave you cross-eyed and frustrated. It's easier to trace all your art on newsprint and arrange on the wall with painter's tape first. Then hang away! For a crisp look use matching frames and all one type of art (i.e., black-and-white photos). For a more eclectic one mix up the finishes and textures of the frames AND what goes inside, including paintings, prints, and even three-dimensional items like antlers!

THE GRID

For this neat and tidy look you will have to get very friendly with your measuring tape and level! Whether it's a triptych or a larger grid, like this one, make sure the frames and mats match in color and size and that all the hanging mechanisms on the back are the same height. Wide mats look fantastic hung this way, as do a series of black-and-white photographs. For smaller frame sizes try to keep about 1 to 2 inches between the frames. For larger pieces you can go up to 4 inches. The distance between pieces should be the same on all sides.

THE BOOKWORM

Hanging art ON bookshelves is an amazing way to break up the business of lots of books. Easiest on built-ins, you can also implement this on single bookcases using small adhesive hooks instead of nails. Pick the art to work with the scale of your bookcase—larger for built-ins that go to the ceiling or span the whole wall, smaller for freestanding pieces.

THE FINE MIX

Mixing artistic mediums can result in a very cool aesthetic, like leaning a large framed print against a mirror or pairing a traditional landscape with a large abstract painting. This application really shines when styling your mantel, so take it a step further by mixing sculptural objects in front of your layered artwork too! Grouping opposing mediums makes for a fantastic contrast and adding artistic interest to a large plain mirror in this way really makes your space feel lived in and unique!

THE VERTICAL

Don't ignore the narrow, tall spaces in your home, such as those beside doorways and between windows. Hanging a vertical stack of frames really draws the eye up and creates the impression of a higher ceiling. Hanging items from ceiling to floor can look striking and inspiring—just make sure everything is securely anchored to the wall in case small children and pets are about.

THE BALANCE

Symmetry is your friend in this case. Anchor your arrangement with one large piece in the center. A large mirror works really well, as does a large-scale piece of art. Be sure to balance the look with a matching arrangement (in scale and medium) on both sides, or ALL sides if you have the space and want the drama! This is a great way to add more interest to a single large item.

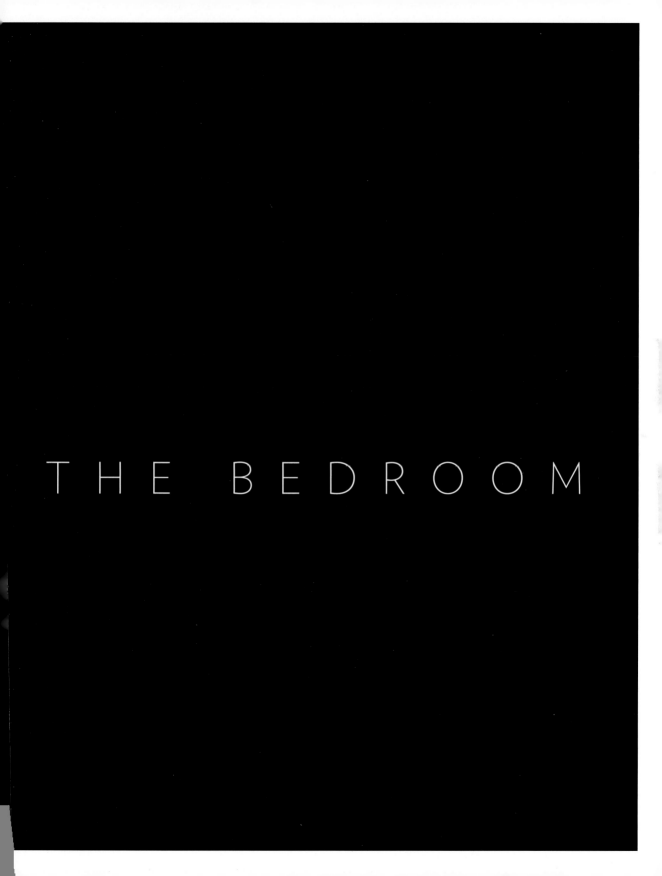

THE BEDROOM

LOVE AND THROW PILLOWS

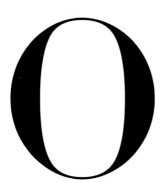ne of the worst fights of my marriage was over a Lucite side table. I never knew the transparent material was so polarizing, but as I learned over a heated dinner at our local Mexican joint, it can drive you to sleep in separate beds. See, I love the way a Lucite piece here and there adds modern glamour to an otherwise traditional space such as our living room. Apparently my husband thought it would transform our home into a replica of the set of *Miami Vice*.

After moving into our second city condo three years into our marriage, we were sipping sangria and debating my request to add such a table to the house. I figured that Andrew, a straight male who spends most weekends screaming at various sporting

OPPOSITE: I wanted my bedroom to be soothing and classic. Refinished side tables given to me by a client (score!) and an upholstered platform bed sit atop a blush overdyed rug. The walls are painted in Benjamin Moore San Antonio Gray.

events on television, would not only not care but not even know what Lucite was. Well, he did, on both counts, and told me in no uncertain terms that we were not going to have any Lucite in our house. It apparently upset him to such an intense degree that his face started resembling the sangria. Which upset me to an intense degree because my job involves designing homes and our home was my laboratory and showroom! Did he not care about my job? Did he not trust me to design a beautiful home for us? Was a little table so offensive that it was worth fighting over? He argued that he shouldn't have to live with something he hated so much. I said he'd barely see it. It IS clear, after all. We went back and forth, the volume and intensity of our voices building with each cocktail until finally I got so mad I slammed my drink down and stormed out of the restaurant tossing a few choice expletives his way while clearly startling our waitress.

And then, as I burst out onto the sidewalk in a rage, I remembered the car was with the valet and I had nowhere to storm off to. Nerds.

We obviously worked through our little design conundrum, and I can gleefully say I now have not one but TWO Lucite tables in my house. And guess who actually likes them? That's right, Mr. I Hate Lucite himself. But this little spat brought up an excellent point about design: it's not just about you, it's about your whole family or whomever you chose to cohabitate with. And if you are anything like my husband and me, you've chosen to share four walls with someone quite different from you.

Andrew and I are total opposites. He's a "glass is half full" kind of guy and I'm more of a "my glass is not only half empty but it's also ugly and so much less stylish than everyone else's glasses" type of gal. We approach life and love in very different ways, a balance that can be both infuriating and incredibly beneficial. He pushes me to be riskier and less stressed out about the little things, while I bring him down to earth and focus him on concrete goals. But we also struggle to understand how the other person's vision of things can be so, well . . . different.

We've moved many times in our relationship and every time I feel like we each learned a lot from the other. Our first apartment was a tiny, dated rental in Harvard Square in which we were giddy to cohabitate and split the rent equally, which meant a balance of power in the decision-making process. Not that there were many decisions to be made—we couldn't afford anything fancy and since we were young and madly in love, I failed to see the shortcomings of our dusty little apartment. It was simply too much fun playing house with my first real, live-in boyfriend. It felt so amazing to be such an "adult" that I didn't care about the laminate countertops, cabinets clearly from the '80s, mirrored closet doors, and lack of dishwasher. Washing dishes together was adorable and fun . . . wouldn't it always be? (My future self is laughing hysterically and pointing.)

We got engaged and decided to buy our first condo together BEFORE making it legal, a concept most parents would balk at and certainly one we had to hide from my rather old-fashioned grandmother until our wedding day. Again, the newness of our first "home" accompanied by the blinding glare of my diamond left us blissfully happy—even in only 700 square feet. We had a dishwasher, a Jacuzzi, and granite counters—what more could we ask for? But a mortgage and new last name began adding stress to our relationship and things started to feel real. I began associating our "stuff" with the state of our marriage, and fights became more frequent, typically about something silly like why we couldn't afford a tufted headboard.

Our next home almost did us in. Instead of enjoying our child-free, newlywed days by moving even closer to the heart of the city like we wanted, we instead bought a bigger condo farther on the outskirts of the city "just in case" we started a family and so I could have a separate office space for my burgeoning design business. This turned out to be one of the biggest mistakes we made: it put too much pressure on us financially AND we had to deal with incredibly loud upstairs neighbors who left me in tears most nights (how can a small child running sound so much like a water buffalo? How?). After not one but two job losses for Andrew, our stresses quickly turned into the perfect storm. We were unhappy on so many fronts—with ourselves, each other, and our house. The "divorce" word crept into our vocabulary. Ironically during this horrible time, I had managed to decorate the space in such a way that it won me my first big break: a shoot for the *Boston Globe Magazine* that ended up on the cover, rocketing my business into profitability. The home was both a blessing and a curse, and through the heartache and joy we experienced while inside those walls we became closer, smarter, and successful. And then finally we plunked a big old FOR SALE sign in the front yard, because sometimes you have to just cut your losses and move on. But not without packing up those tough life lessons to bring along with you.

We've now been married nine years. And in that time we've created a life uniquely ours that is far from perfect but full of interesting twists and turns. Our new home certainly reflects our journey together—from the antiques we inherited from Andrew's wonderful grandparents to an estate sale find I literally made him guard with his body as I ran full speed to an ATM

ABOVE: I found the wallpaper panels online and framed them, thus adding much-needed height to our low-ceilinged room. I mixed gold frames with nickel lighting and nailheads to keep things from feeling too matchy.

OPPOSITE: Needing to conserve money in our budget, I added heavy brass hardware to an Ikea dresser and painted a canvas for the wall in tones used in the room. No one can say I haven't put my bachelor's degree to use!

to get cash. We have art on our walls that I've painted and a gallery wall collecting images of our favorite people and times in our life, and the layout of our new kitchen and addition is the first design collaboration between my dad and me. I love that our space tells a story, but that doesn't mean it's a cakewalk to make it a space both Andrew and I love. Through all my client work and the many homes I myself have lived in, I've learned the secret to marital decorating success: NEGOTIATION.

In my years of working with couples I've come to realize that most men have few design needs beyond a comfy place to sit and the biggest TV that can possibly fit on the wall. Oh, and they categorically do not like chairs without arms, Lucite (I think we've already covered THAT one), tulip tables, and the color pink. Some rare birds, however, want to be a part of the decision-making process every step of the way. Which is tough when you have one person wanting French country and the other midcentury modern. But mixing styles can create a look all your own—a big leather chair here offset by a linen slip-covered sofa there can look great together! It's all about the art of give and take, like other parts of relationships. When I decided I really, really wanted a bold leopard runner on our stairs, Andrew's first reaction was negative. I believe his exact reaction was "HELL NO." But then I reminded him that he put a nice big TV above the fireplace, against my better judgment, and all of a sudden we had a deal. And my joy walking up the stairs masks the pain I feel looking at that big black box above the mantel.

You have to listen to your partner's wishes, no matter how much you want them to butt out and leave it to you or your designer. This is a HOME, not a showroom, and the spaces you live in need to work for everyone and make you all feel like you are reflected in the choices made. There will be things you won't like—for me it's the ugly file cabinets in the office and the damn TV. There will be LOTS of things he won't like (for Andrew it's mostly the obscene amount of throw pillows I have everywhere and the fact that I refuse to get anything but white duvets, even though the dogs ruin them in a matter of weeks). Granted, living with a designer who uses her house as a showpiece leaves poor Andrew with a lot less bargaining room than most men. But one day I hope to give him his own man cave, resplendent with a Ping-Pong table, leather sofa, and surround sound, leaving the rest of the house for me to fill with Lucite and inappropriate upholstery. The give-and-take we practice while designing a house seems to be the same as that of "designing" a life together. There are ups and downs and when we can, we soften the blows with a few good throw pillows.

ABOVE LEFT: I had custom monograms added to store-bought shams.

ABOVE RIGHT: A mix of accessories
livens up the dresser.

BEAUTY IN THE BEDROOM

Whether it's your master or a guestroom, the bedroom is a place where people want to feel relaxed and soothed. This doesn't mean it has to be boring. Maybe the color red soothes you . . . it's not for me to judge, but overall I like to approach bedrooms with sleep in mind. Typically that results in light and clean color palettes and lots of softness. Comfort and luxury go a long way in the bedroom, so be smart about where you spend and where you save.

A FIRM FOUNDATION

The bed takes up most of the space and attention in a bedroom, so make sure it's worthwhile. Headboard and bed types vary greatly. Upholstered ones are great for reading or watching TV in bed but they can get soiled easily. Wood-framed beds and headboards are sturdy and classic but not quite as comfy. But what matters most is a great mattress. Don't skimp here: be sure to spend well on the one thing in your bedroom you'll spend the most time on and that will help you get your best night's sleep!

OPPOSITE: Our guestroom is one of my favorite spaces. The lightest pink (Benjamin Moore Blanched Coral) covers the walls, but the femininity is toned down with graphic black-and-white accents. Affordable finds are everywhere in this room!

DEFINE YOUR STYLE: BEDROOM

modern

Graphic four-poster bed, abstract art, chrome, and glass.

eclectic

Linen upholstery, bohemian rugs, ceramic lamps, and block prints.

  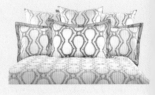

glamorous

Tufted headboard, chinoiserie panels, shag rugs, and crystal.

traditional

Wood framed bed, landscape art, monograms, and florals.

new country

Turned-wood bed, wool blankets, antlers, and jute.

OPPOSITE: An old family hand-me-down dresser got a fresh coat of black paint for its move into this room. Hanging above it, another homemade abstract work of art layered with more traditional finds.

CLOCKWISE FROM TOP LEFT: Fresh towels for guests are kept in a basket under the mirrored console. Mixing both glamorous and rustic textures works well. • A tufted chair bought on a flash-sale website holds an edgy snake pillow that keeps the room from being too girly. I mounted and framed a set of vintage car keys I found in an antique shop. • A new spot for our modern bookshelves offers guests lots to choose from for a bedtime read.

AVOID MY BIGGEST PET PEEVE: TOO-LOW DRAPES

One tip I repeat incessantly to anyone who will listen is to always, ALWAYS hang your drapes as close to the ceiling as possible! Placing the curtain rod high makes your ceilings look taller than they are, and if you already have high ceilings, it makes them look even MORE dramatic. I cannot emphasize this enough! Also, install your rods wide enough so that the drapes hang mostly over wall space instead of covering the actual window. You want as much natural light as possible to come into your home!

OPPOSITE: I love this coral, tan, and white combination we used in a small condo bedroom. The built-ins were papered with grass cloth to add texture, and the headboard is custom-made in a gorgeous velvet.

ABOVE, LEFT TO RIGHT: A warm combination of texture, color, and pattern. Swing-arm sconces allow for ideal reading light. • Lots of layering in this bedroom, from the area rug over the wall-to-wall carpet to the drapes layered over blackout woven wood shades.

READY TO READ

I love to finish my day by reading in bed. Good lighting next to the bed is crucial for this purpose, and you have a slew of options to choose from. Swing-arm sconces are a great choice for keeping valuable real estate available on your nightstand for books, water, and alarm clocks. The sconces' adjustability gives you the exact amount of light you need. However, they do not illuminate a whole room, so avoid these if you have no other source of light. A pair of matching bedside lamps always makes a statement and is a great place to introduce color into your bedroom. Make sure they are tall enough to complement your headboard height, but not so tall that you have to get out of bed to turn them off.

OPPOSITE: Light blue is a popular bedroom color for traditional designs. Here, it's made modern with clean lines, a restrained palette, and interesting details.

ABOVE, LEFT TO RIGHT: The Lucite legs on this tufted bench are simply everything! • A gilded mirror and Buddha statue introduce metallic elements to this bedroom and look great paired with the rough texture of the dresser.

BEDDING DOWN

There is a lot of conflicting advice when it comes to things like thread count and fancy bedding. My advice? Buy the nicest you can afford, as long as they are natural cotton or linen, and don't sweat the thread count. When it comes to dressing the bed, I really like to mix it up: contrasting patterned or colored shams with a simple bordered white duvet set and another variation of sheets looks great and more personal than an entire matching set.

ABOVE: Painterly wallpaper and fretwork details on a built-in.

OPPOSITE: The dramatic ceiling in this bedroom gave us ample space to create an accent wall with a scenic wallpaper. Built-in bookshelves were designed to house the owner's massive collection of books, and a custom headboard anchors the space.

LEFT: We decided to go bold with a patterned custom headboard in this guest suite. A statement flush-mount fixture keeps the eye interested, as do the touches of bright yellow. The nightstand serves as a desk as well.

OPPOSITE, LEFT TO RIGHT: The bedroom of an old apartment of mine that was a bit of a departure for me. Bright color mixed with deep gray walls and a worn Persian rug (found on eBay) made for a happy little haven. • This airy penthouse-level bedroom benefits from a vaulted ceiling and a canopy bed that accentuates the amazing light and loft!

A GREAT GUESTROOM

Having guests spend the night can be stressful for you—and them! No one wants to feel awkward tiptoeing around the house in their pajamas trying to figure out where towels or the coffeemaker are. Having a nicely prepared and stocked guestroom guarantees your guests will feel right at home. Some items I love to include in my guestroom are:

A BASKET WITH FRESH TOWELS and a small toiletry bag containing travel-size shampoo, conditioner, lotion, and cotton balls.

AN EXTRA BLANKET in case they get cold.

A CARAFE OF FRESH WATER WITH A GLASS (add a slice of lemon or fresh cucumber to really impress them).

A SMALL TRAY WITH TRAVEL ESSENTIALS: aspirin, a couple of Band-Aids, a toothbrush and small toothpaste, a mini stain stick, a disposable razor, small scissors, and some hair elastics.

A SCENTED CANDLE AND MATCHES.

A MINIATURE KEURIG COFFEE BREWER, MUGS, SPOONS, AND SUGAR. It's so nice to have a little coffee before getting dressed!

OPPOSITE, CLOCKWISE FROM TOP: Vintage wallpaper panels were the jumping-off point for the color scheme in this large and serene bedroom. • We used a modern chaise to create a fun little reading area in a formerly unused corner of this large bedroom. • Pairing some hip accessories with a statement mirror makes this hardworking large traditional dresser more interesting.

ABOVE: The mix of wood, glass, soft linen, and metals creates a harmonious blend.

A guestroom done in tones of blue and gray, with a geometric area rug for fun. • Applying trim with some pattern to white window treatments is an easy and classic detail in any room.

OPPOSITE, CLOCKWISE FROM TOP LEFT: A quiet moment in a well-equipped window seat. • A large tray keeps guestroom essentials neat and tidy, while this gold mirror makes for a gorgeous place to check your lipstick. • An existing bedroom set is made more youthful with bedding and art in a modern print.

ABOVE: Grass-cloth-covered walls envelop you in this bedroom, and the red-and-turquoise accents warm it up even further.

ABOVE: This leather-and-wood paneled dresser adds a contemporary flair to an otherwise traditional space.

WHY DO WE NEED SO MANY PILLOWS?

It's the question every man asks—just why do we need so many pillows on the bed? It's a good question, especially if it takes half an hour to make your bed every morning. Here is an illustrated guide to styling any size of bed, and it can double as backup to your argument about why you absolutely need that new bolster!

TWIN

One sleeping pillow

One standard sham

One 18-inch square decorative pillow

FULL

One or two sleeping pillows

Two standard shams

One bolster pillow or two 18-inch square decorative pillows

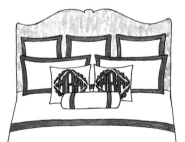

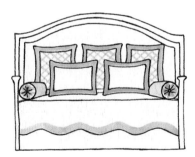

QUEEN

Two sleeping pillows

Two Euro shams

Two standard shams

One large bolster or two 20-inch decorative pillows

KING

Two king sleeping pillows

Three Euro shams

Two king shams

One large bolster or two 20-inch decorative pillows

DAYBED

Two sleeping pillows

Three Euro shams

Two standard shams or 20-inch square decorative pillows

Two long round bolster pillows for ends

A small guestroom in a city condo features a trundle bed decked out in coral and light turquoise. The sconces free up valuable space on the small nightstand.

THE BATHROOM

REFLECTIONS ON BEAUTY

When facing my bathroom mirror every day, I am reminded that beauty, and the perception of it, is something that has become central to my own feelings of self-worth. I have struggled with this my entire life. I also put too much importance on my own appearance and let it greatly affect my mood and even occasionally my work. I feel like I have to look perfect all the time, rarely leaving the house without an application of makeup and an outfit I wouldn't mind being buried in. But this was not always the case. . . .

You see, I was not a cute adolescent. People who did not know me then like to argue with me about this. Let me assure you I was not. Let me assure you even further still.

OPPOSITE: My custom vanity provides tons of storage in the single full bathroom in our house. The black walls (Benjamin Moore Space Black) were a challenge to get approved by other members of the household (ahem!), but are now loved by all!

I'll give you a minute to take it all in while I go hyperventilate into a paper bag over the fact that I just published that picture for the entire world (and all my ex-boyfriends) to see. Where shall I begin? The walrus teeth? The unibrow? The extraordinary mullet topped off by the world's ugliest headband? Or perhaps the collision of chubbiness and my spectacular '80s clothing (I wore that sweatshirt in TWO professional photos that year, TWO!). My mother still insists I was "so cute" while my dad is more realistic in saying, "People will think you've had plastic surgery." Even my husband, who is the first to pay me lavish compliments, looks at photos from this era and stifles a laugh.

Want to know the funny thing, though? At this age, I thought I was awesome. I believe I even told my mom I wanted to be a teen model and made her take headshots of me. My confidence knew no bounds, and my mom deserves an Academy Award for not dying of laughter as I tried to get that mullet to flow in the breeze.

I never thought about calories, clothing size, comparing myself to other girls, or waxing (even though I was more Teen Wolf than teen model material). I wouldn't think twice when absolutely crushing a Croissan'wich at Burger King on Sunday mornings (as in every Sunday), or fret when I needed to go up a size in my Limited Too cranberry-colored jeans. I was me, and there was no other "me" out there, so why would I be worried? My appearance, beyond copying Blossom's illustrious fashions, was not of the utmost importance. Puffy painting everything within my grasp and finding my brother the perfect bridesmaid outfit to go with my dress-up wedding gown were of more concern.

And then one day things changed. And I don't really know why or how. I could blame the media or my genetics or social pressure (there are only so many times you can not be asked to dance by a boy at a school function until it starts hurting and changing you), but I can't pinpoint a specific aha moment or traumatic taunt by a peer. But suddenly I started to worry, compare, and diet. I began to try to "fix" myself, and once I started, it spread through me like a flame on an oil slick. I began to hate my body, hate my face, hate that I wasn't cool, hate that I felt invisible, hate that I wasn't perfect. And that hatred fueled a near-death battle with anorexia that left me a ravaged shell of skin and bones and locked up in a mental hospital insisting I looked normal and that everyone ELSE was crazy. The hard part to explain (and fathom) was that I did think I looked totally fine and I did think that eating 250 calories a day was totally healthy. At five foot nine and ninety-five pounds, I assure you I looked anything BUT healthy. I could have easily passed for the Crypt Keeper.

But this is how and when my body dysmorphic disorder developed, and I now have to admit, it's never left. Recently I was asked to contribute to a book about recovering from eating disorders, and while reading it, I realized I am still not out of the woods. I'm not sure I ever completely will be. I feel so far less confident and happy with how I look now than when I was that pudgy little bucktoothed girl of eleven, but I'm not sick like I was either. Inside I am still the girl no one asked to dance and I always will be, no matter how much the outside of me changes. Until I read that book, I assumed that the BDD had been beaten alongside the anorexia, like two evil culprits linked arm in arm, skulking off in the night. But these things do not always exist only together. One of them can linger and even hide for a while, only to resurface when it senses the slightest loosening of recovery's grasp. So while I now eat with abandon, I still hate looking in the mirror because I cannot do it without being fiercely critical. The reflection I see is vastly different

from what others see—something many doctors have corroborated.

The hardest part is that people think I am exhibiting false modesty or fishing for compliments, when really I'm reflecting from a far darker, sadder place. I've turned down TV shows for this reason, shied away from photo shoots and stopped posting the "What I'm Wearing" segment on my blog that so many readers loved to see. The blogosphere already perpetuates the concept of perfection on so many levels. I certainly find that I feel bad

ABOVE: The small details, like flowers in a gorgeous vase on the vanity, help start your day off right.

about myself when I peruse too many blogs that focus solely on appearance. So I found that opening myself up to public criticism based on how I look was sending me many, many steps back in my lifelong desire for self-acceptance and to value the internal over the external. This struggle is frustrating for those who care about me, and it's torture for me to live with. But I AM working on it. And I hope that someday not only will I like what I see but, more important, I WON'T CARE.

In fact, in the past couple of years I've gritted my teeth and participated in photo shoots for magazines and even filmed an ad for TV. When the director of the ad came over to show me footage of what we'd just filmed, I leaped away like I was taking on sniper fire. I can get myself to do these things. I just don't want to see them. For the same reason, I still do not know how much I weigh. I turn around at the doctor's office and ask them not to tell me. In fact, a version of this essay was published in a major magazine and, ironically enough, the picture they shot to run with it was really bad. And not just by my standards, but by others' as well. Instead of being hysterical and horrified, I kept telling myself to focus on the fact that I was a published writer. My appearance was not what it was all about (even if the story was!). It was a small step in the right direction and a lesson I remind myself of every day. And as I get older and start dealing with gray hairs

and deepened smile lines, those lessons apply even more.

Not everyone has such an extreme relationship with their appearance, but I have yet to meet a woman who is 100 percent confident in every inch of her body or face—just look at the money being made on cosmetics, creams, procedures, and diets and makeover TV shows ("Plastic surgery for EVERYONE!"). I know that so many people have similar feelings they may not like to acknowledge or talk about with others. But admitting them is the first step to overcoming them. So here I am, publishing one of my worst pictures in an attempt to hold myself accountable to be stronger and continue to work harder and fight the fight with every passing day.

But you know what? I am grateful I went through that awkward phase, if only because it served as inspiration for the most epic father-of-the-bride speech ever given, in which my dad recounted getting a call from me from a pay phone at my middle school, crying because no one would dance with me. He came to pick me up and took me home and promised me that someday all the boys would want to dance with me, but until then he would dance anytime I wanted. And as I stood there some fourteen years later, finally a bride for real, next to the man who wanted to dance all his dances with me, he pulled out a roll of what he called "Daddy's Dance Tickets with Erin" and

LEFT: We kept the existing tile and cast-iron tub, reglazing them bright white instead of spending the money to rip out and replace. It was a huge budget saver!

before

gave them to Andrew, saying he was the only man he trusted to be my lifelong dance partner. But as he handed them over he tore one ticket off and looked at me and said, "But I get one last dance." I would not have traded being the most popular and beautiful middle school girl in the world for that moment. I wouldn't trade anything for that moment, in fact, and as I look at that picture I have hated and hidden for so many years I feel nothing but love for that silly bucktoothed girl and know that she is going to be okay.

NO, I KNOW THAT SHE IS OKAY.

MAKING YOUR BATHROOM GORGEOUS

BE MINDFUL OF LIGHTING

It's the most important thing in a bathroom. You need great lighting for your makeup application and his shaving (we don't want any bloodshed!). Sconces mounted on the sides of your mirror illuminate best as long as they are strong enough (check the wattage—you want 60 watts or more per sconce). If your only option is a sconce above the mirror, use one with multiple lights and shades that face up instead of down to avoid downcast lighting (having dark circles amplified does no one any favors!).

MIRROR, MIRROR . . .

Speaking of mirrors, don't only select one (or two) standard bathroom mirrors. Consider regular, decoratively framed wall mirrors too for a more interesting look (as I did in my bathroom). Be sure to measure the space above your sink for the right fit, and think about where you will store the items you would have otherwise kept in a medicine cabinet. If storage is an issue in your bathroom, you can find medicine cabinets with decorative edges and frames that make them look less utilitarian.

OPPOSITE: I love how this vintage framed sketch looks against the deep-black walls. Slightly unexpected and glamorous in such a utilitarian space.

LEFT: Keeping color schemes light and bright in bathrooms, like this gray-and-white one, creates a spalike feel. The print, as opposed to color, adds interest.

BELOW: We custom designed this large built-in vanity and found an adorable vanity chair to complement it.

OPPOSITE: The pattern on this sheer mimics the shape of the vanity chair opposite, and the hint of blue on the recessed ceiling adds a bit of color to an otherwise monochromatic space.

COLOR IS CRUCIAL

Saturated colors such as green and blue will bounce off your skin, making you look less than your best. Neutrals, pale shades, and pinks are wonderful choices that improve your glow. Going black, as I did, is fun but does absorb more light, so amp up the wattage on your fixtures if you go to the dark side!

ABOVE, LEFT TO RIGHT: A serene and feminine guest bathroom. • An angular modern bathroom gets a touch of traditional pattern by way of a paisley block-print wallpaper.

GROUT GRIPES

Choosing white grout to go in between my floor tiles was a mistake I'll never make again! Over time bright white looks dingy on such a hard-wearing application, so go with a slightly darker gray or tan.

ABOVE, LEFT TO RIGHT: Sparkly pendants and a custom-lacquered frame mirror create a feminine and functional master bathroom. • Our client's preppy powder room is decked out in orange-printed grass cloth. The paintings hung outside the space relate beautifully with the color scheme.

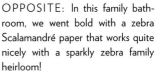

OPPOSITE: In this family bathroom, we went bold with a zebra Scalamandré paper that works quite nicely with a sparkly zebra family heirloom!

LEFT: A simple and bright master bathroom is finished off with a patterned cornice and gray woven wood Roman shades. A little pop of yellow enlivens the space.

LISTEN TO YOUR MOTHER

My mom told me I should install a shower with a removable handheld head for easier cleaning. Did I listen to her? No. Do I wish I had? Yes. Especially when trying to figure out how to get the soapsuds off the shower walls when I'm trying to clean them.

GO CRAZY

With wallpaper, that is. The powder room is the PERFECT small space to take a chance and do something bolder than you would in a more public room. Clients who have done this end up loving those rooms the most! But if you are installing wallpaper in a bathroom with a shower, use vinyl paper or have it professionally installed by someone in the know. Peeling wallpaper isn't a good look on anyone.

before

ABOVE LEFT: I love small details, such as the script on the faucet handles.

OPPOSITE: My powder room is positively minuscule, so by applying a busy David Hicks patterned wallpaper, the edges of the room are blurred. We replaced everything; new fixtures include a teeny-tiny pedestal sink. While my husband finds this wallpaper dizzying, I positively adore it. The faux Roman valance and sheer roller shade provide privacy and a finishing touch.

THIS PAGE, CLOCKWISE FROM TOP
LEFT: Powder rooms are the best places to have
some fun, like with this ostrich wallpaper. Offset the
quirkiness with more traditional accents. • A jewel-
box-like powder room we redid in a metallic paper
is complemented by a Venetian-style mirror and a
repainted vanity. • Our stylish client implemented
this scheme all on her own—the tree wallpaper and
amazing fretwork paneling create a scheme that is
beyond fun!

OPPOSITE: A bold and truly fun powder room.
We skirted the pedestal sink to allow for some concealed storage.

renter's tip

Bad bathrooms in apartments are such a bummer. I've had to live with a couple doozies myself. A great way to detract from bad tile and old tubs is to install a bold-patterned shower curtain, lay down a small area rug instead of a bath mat to cover the floor, and, when allowed, paint. Old pink and black tiles can look retro-chic when the walls are painted black!

SPALIKE TOUCHES

You can make even a tiny bathroom feel luxurious with the right accessories. Plush white towels (add a monogram for an even MORE fabulous touch), scented candles (only clean, crisp scents, please), decorative containers for makeup brushes, razors, and toothbrushes, and a piece of beautiful artwork will improve even the dingiest bathroom!

ABOVE: Horizontally striped wall covering and a new coat of gray paint on the existing vanity took this guest bathroom from boring to bold. A Roman shade trimmed in a similar colorway finishes off the space.

OPPOSITE: A favorite powder room of mine, the mirror reflects one long wall papered in a Katie Ridder print.

THE NURSERY

THE BIG BABY

I was out shopping for a baby shower gift a couple of years ago and as I was perusing a very lovely but VERY pricey baby boutique (with Andrew yelling from across the store "This baby sweater is a hundred and ninety-five bucks! *I* don't have a hundred-and-ninety-five-dollar sweater! What the hell!?"), I saw it. The embroidered baby sling that made my tummy do flip-flops of joy. I had coveted it before online but had not yet seen it in person. I picked it up and inspected the lovely detailing and then, to my horror, held it up to myself. "Trying it on," if you will. I looked at Andrew and said, "I think I might buy it." He assumed I meant as a gift for one of my pregnant friends but, no, I meant for a very unpregnant me.

OPPOSITE: Fit for a princess, this custom canopy for a store-bought daybed is the stuff little girls' dreams are made of.

This happened again in the not so distant past when Diane von Furstenberg designed a limited edition line of children's clothing, including miniature printed wrap dresses. DVF wrap dresses are my signature item of clothing, so I quickly added one to my online cart, not even knowing what kid size to order, and clicked purchase. I found myself cautiously looking over my shoulder trying to protect my screen from anyone seeing and then giving me that I'm-sorry-you're-so-crazy look. I get that a lot.

The thing is, I've spent the last five years of my life (and marriage) wondering if I even WANT kids. Clearly I like the accoutrements that come with them and would find it delightful to have a mini-me or mini-he to dress up—but I am not entirely sure I'm ready for the honest to goodness, difficult and dirty details of motherhood. It's a HUGE decision, the biggest I can imagine having to make—being responsible for the health, well-being, and sanity of another human being—and one I do not take lightly. Yet everyone and their mother (mine and Andrew's included) seems to think it's okay to ask me AD NAUSEUM the one question every childless thirtysomething doesn't want to hear and yet fields almost daily:

"When are you going to have kids?"

I get asked that question a lot these days, especially after telling people that I've been

married eight years. Hardly a child bride, but young by the standards set by my peers, I was one of the first to walk down the aisle and now one of the last to be pushed into the delivery room. This unnerves people, the bewilderment spreading across their faces as they try to comprehend why I don't have a bundle of joy yet.

Recently I have realized what a tumultuous time the thirties are for women. It's the decade of SO much change in our lives. In one set of friends you can have one person with three kids, some pregnant, a handful childless, others not even engaged yet, and some even ending their marriages. This diversity in lifestyles and milestones causes a tough dynamic between women that seems to get swept under the table because it's simply too uncomfortable to discuss. It's such an emotionally charged decade to navigate, full of joy, sadness, excitement, jealousy, and yearning. And just when you think you have it all figured out, for the twenty-fourth time in one month, a friend announces her pregnancy on Facebook. A little snapshot of a sonogram that fills you with both happiness and yet a pang of loss and you begin to think *maybe I've got it all wrong.* Instead of reveling in your successes, you feel like a

OPPOSITE: A chair and a half serves as the perfect spot for this little girl to read with her mom.

failure as you zero in on the one thing missing in your life. And you may not even WANT it yet, but for some reason you feel you SHOULD want it . . . paging the shrink.

The truth is, I have been trying to get pregnant on and off for the past few years. And it's clearly just not happening for me right now. Medically, we are healthy as horses, but the universe has just decided it's not time yet. A smart universe, I might add, as I have had this friggin' BOOK to give birth to (which probably causes a similar amount of pain, I imagine, as birthing a human). My incredibly busy schedule has kept me from feeling I was missing out, and also from starting any fertility treatment. I have a lot to accomplish and I can't be sick or distracted while I'm crossing this big item off my bucket list. The smart part of me says, *Erin, one thing at a time, you'll be a better mother if you succeed in accomplishing goals for yourself first.* But then the other part of me feels so left out and that time is ticking for us. My eggs can't be the freshest in the lot, and Andrew celebrated his fortieth birthday a year ago (although I think he's still the emotional age of about twenty-five). But the honest truth is I've never been the girl who's been just

DYING to have a baby. My biological clock is more like a Swiss watch than a church bell: consistent, but whisper quiet. Our neighborhood's obnoxious teenagers also seem to be serving as a sobering reminder that babies turn into screaming, annoying, angst-y creatures. But even given all that, I know I want to experience motherhood in this lifetime, I very much do. It's just a question of WHEN.

It's hard feeling like the odd girl out. The only one without a baby saddled on her hip. A great job, awesome husband, and beautiful house, yes, but not that one thing that seems to bind women together. It's only natural for mothers, especially new moms, to spend more time with others going through what they are, but I can't help but notice how motherhood sometimes draws a line in the sand between those with kids and those without. People you used to meet for a drink or hang out with seem to disappear from your radar. Dinner dates become fewer. Emails less frequent. It's heartbreaking, yet understandable when it happens. People latch on to those who are experiencing the same things as they are; it's only natural. I'm sure they feel that talking about all the minute details of motherhood would bore those

> INSTEAD OF LOOKING AT THE BOXES LEFT UNCHECKED ON OUR LIFE TO-DO LIST, WE SHOULD BE LOOKING AT THE ONES WE HAVE CHECKED OFF.

of us who aren't going through it, and NOT talking about it would be like trying to write a novel without using vowels. Impossible. So there is a natural separation. And there is also a specifically tough dynamic between those who get pregnant and those who struggle to. Remember how on *Sex and the City* Miranda felt horrible telling Charlotte she was pregnant because Miranda knew Charlotte was having a hard time and it happened to be incredibly easy for her? That happens every day off the TV screen. It's happened to me. I've always thought I was a Carrie, but apparently I'm a Charlotte too.

I have decorated many a nursery during these years of procreation waffling, attempting, and questioning. I absolutely LOVE helping others craft the perfect space to welcome their children into and then spend their formative years in, but it does become hard to do over and over again and never for yourself. In fact, I found the most wonderful fabric for a nursery scheme recently and instead of showing it to clients, I set it aside for myself. Just in case. I hope I don't become that crazy woman amassing a closet full of things for a child I don't have, but I do think it's okay to keep some things just for me in the hopes that I do someday have someone to use them for. But if I start taking dolls out to dinner and forcing

waitresses to take their orders (this happened to me once when waiting tables, believe it or not) call the padded-room people, okay?

And it may not be a baby for you. It may be a ring, or a house, or a job. There is always something that makes you feel your life is not the one you had hoped or planned for. That there is something missing, incomplete, or off. And the thing to remember is that it will ALWAYS be this way no matter what age you are. Instead of looking at the boxes left unchecked on our life to-do list, we should be looking at the ones we HAVE checked off. Everyone's life plan is different, and we miss the joy of what's happening to us right now if we consistently focus on what's not. It's all very zen and namaste of me to say, but we do need to be more present. I need to be more present. Yes, I need to be vigilant about my health and have a plan so that I can make sure I can have a baby someday, but focusing on that is making me miss the wonderful things going on right now, of which there are many.

I AM WHERE I NEED TO BE RIGHT NOW. AND I'LL BE SOMEWHERE ELSE SOON ENOUGH.

MAYBE EVEN WITH A BABY IN TOW.

CRAFTING THE
PERFECT NURSERY

In design you should never say never, but I will about one thing specifically: I will never use a cartoon-character wallpaper border in a child's room.

EVER.

Children's spaces, of course, should not resemble a delicate French drawing room or extreme minimalist living room, but that does not mean you have to go to the other side of the spectrum and decorate with Winnie the Pooh and strictly primary colors. As long as there is a fun, interesting mix of pattern and color, you can make the rooms in your home dedicated to the tiny ones agreeable to adult sensibilities and charming for them too.

We don't have a nursery in our house, obviously. But we have a room earmarked for one. Don't tell me you've never walked through an open house and thought, *well this would be a cute nursery . . . ,* while your significant other throws you the hairy eyeball! The smallest room in our home (as it currently stands) is that room, and we currently are using it as Andrew's office, knowing full well that his desk and filing cabinets will be relegated to the finished basement once I am with child. We have a bigger guestroom too, but I want to keep that for guests, as babies don't need tons of

---

OPPOSITE: The nursery that launched a thousand repins on Pinterest! Reader Jennifer Garran proves that you can create a non-babyish nursery with lots of personality.

space. And our navy walls could serve as a fabulous backdrop to either gender.

One of the most popular nurseries I ever posted on my blog had dark-gray walls. Yes, a very mature and moody charcoal gray. Above the crib hangs a modern abstract painting with great colors and on the crib a skirt of fantastic Josef Frank fabric. A stylish geometric rug skimmed the floor and EVERYONE, I mean EVERYONE, went nuts for this space. You know why? Because it combined the beauty of a classic, non-age-specific design with the functionality of a child-friendly nursery. There are a great mix of colors to attract the attention of baby, but it also is a space YOU would want to hang out in. And let's be honest here—you spend more time conscious in these spaces than the kids do! So why not make it a place where you want to hang out? Midnight feedings are much better when illuminated by a drop-dead table lamp.

RIGHT: This little girl's room has grown along with her nicely—from crib to big-girl bed—and will work even into teen years easily without appearing too juvenile!

OPPOSITE: The China Seas–fabric Romans and storage-nook closet are a personal favorite.

GIRLS

Pick a bold but girly large-scale print for window treatments and ponder pairing a traditional color, like purple, with an unexpected one, like this bold green.

Make the color pink pop by combining this sweet tone with animal prints and fantastic natural textures like grass cloth (use the vinyl version for easy cleanup) and a shag rug with tones of brown.

BOYS

Orange and navy is a fantastic color combination that looks cheerful and modern. Mix traditional "boy" prints like boats with hip geometric patterns and touches of leather!

Blue and green is classic, but can be totally hip too. An accent wall in a fun wallpaper, like this sailboat pattern, mixed with bold stripes and modern prints will make for a space you and your little man will love.

IT'S A SURPRISE

Graphic black and white is a great place to start when you don't know if you are having a boy or girl. Touches of emerald green are great for either gender and allow you to mix in gender-specific details once the little one is born.

Citron yellow is a spunkier alternative to this popular neutral. Mixing a geometric print with a sweet bunny-themed wallpaper and anchoring the room with gray tones is both soothing and fun.

THE NONBABYISH NURSERY

When planning your nursery, don't limit yourself to looking at stores and sites dedicated only to nursery décor. While you will have to buy certain items at those stores (cribs, bedding, and the like), others you can source from various places like vintage shops and regular furniture stores. We've used adult-sized dressers as changing tables, vintage chairs as rockers, and modern art to decorate the walls of small-people spaces! Making this room one you enjoy as much as your child does is important—you want to love the space you spend so many sleepless nights in, after all!

COLOR SCHEMES

Girls don't have to be pink. Boys don't have to be blue. I love navy or gray walls for either gender as a super-chic base. For girls, add pops of coral, and for boys, consider burnt orange (think Hermès) or emerald green. And do not overlook wallpaper in this case. A single wall of amazing pattern (even the ceiling) is such a playful touch. And don't fret about it being precious—many fabulous prints and textures come in easy-to-clean vinyl.

ABOVE: We took a bold approach to this little boy's room, pairing a Katie Ridder sailboat wallpaper with bright turquoise walls. Even his puppy loves it!

RIGHT, TOP TO BOTTOM: We layered two different grosgrain ribbons as trim on the geometric print Roman shades. • Animal silhouettes were cut out of paper and mounted on vintage wallpaper inside store-bought frames as budget-friendly art.

In this tiny room, we created a modern and bright nursery by painting orange-and-white stripes on the ceiling, the walls Benjamin Moore's Little Piggy, and keeping the rest of the furniture white.

OPPOSITE: A pink-and-navy room features a daybed full of cheerful pillows, overdyed rug, and Roman shades with bold pink trim.

LEFT: We found this vintage armoire in Palm Beach and had it refinished in white and navy as a perfect storage piece.

renter's tip

Custom window treatments might feel like a waste of money in a space that isn't permanent, but thankfully there are retail sources that sell premade blackout Roman shades perfect for a nursery. Outside-mount styles are best for this noncustom item, and I like to install them above the top window molding to give the room a little height.

FURNITURE FROM BEYOND

Yes, cribs should come from reputable children's furniture stores for safety reasons (and need not be expensive: I've used some great, stylish ones from Ikea and Walmart too). But for other pieces consider vintage items or those from chic adult sources. Almost anything can be a changing table if you pop a changing console on top, such as a Dorothy Draper–style chest or a designer dresser. I've seen some killer midcentury rocking chairs used instead of gliders as well. Try thinking outside the baby catalog box and you'll be surprised how incredible it looks.

OPPOSITE: A pair of vintage bamboo headboards was paired with custom ikat bedskirts in this happy turquoise-and-orange room. The walls are painted in C2 Hush.

ABOVE: An older child's room is playful yet mature with its scenic accent wall and pink upholstered headboard.

LET'S GET REAL

I know every parent swears up and down at some point in their early days that they will NOT have their homes littered with blinking, singing, and moving plastic toys. Instead, they promise to have only chic, wooden French trinkets for their little ones to entertain themselves with. This usually goes to pot within a few months when the only thing that will keep the kid quiet and happy happens to take AA batteries and is the size of a Volkswagen. You will have to allow some ugly things into the space, but please don't let them take over everything. Have an organization plan in place so you can clean up quickly and the kids can access what they want easily. If you have enough space to do so, contain toys and kid stuff in a separate room and keep Elmo out of your living room. Mommy needs her own dedicated space too.

OPPOSITE, CLOCKWISE FROM TOP LEFT: In this twin girls' nursery, a feminine daybed serves as a place for parents to nap or watch over the babies. • We designed custom crib skirts and a small gallery wall to unite the two cribs. • Teeny dresses can make adorable decorative accessories! • Knockout print drapes in an older child's room really take the cake.

THE OFFICE

ADVENTURES IN BLOG LAND

When I was a little girl, all I wanted to be was a checkout lady in the grocery store. The allure of being in charge of a cash register and wielding the mighty power of the scanner gun was my ultimate in employment dreams. But then I grew up and thought that maybe, just maybe, I was destined for something greater. I had a unique exposure to the field of fashion and design in my childhood, through my family's involvement in fashion and architecture. I got to spend lots of time parked high up at a drafting desk in my dad's office drawing "floor plans" or wandering around our family store fingering racks of clothing and fogging up the jewelry counter as I ogled the bling (which I now

OPPOSITE: While not a home office, the previous office space for my design company offers up home-like accents such as this vintage dining set repurposed as a conference table.

know was all costume jewelry, but to a little kid it looked like the Queen of England's finest possessions).

Being an indecisive person my whole life, though, I still could not commit to a major when I arrived on my college campus. I did, however, manage to be the only girl in my dorm to hang curtains and finagle a pleated bed skirt onto her crappy futon. A sign, perhaps, of what the future would hold for me. I toyed around with psychology as a focus, but quickly did a U-turn back to what I knew was my true passion—art. I'm sure many a parent thinks, *just what is my kid going to do with a bachelor's degree in painting?* Well, let me tell you what they will do. Flounder at a few jobs and feel ungratified until they finally decide to make their own careers. At least that's what I did.

My first job after college was in an art gallery on Boston's famed Newbury Street. I loved the gallery life, being surrounded by gorgeous works of art all day, but a natural salesgirl I was not. When the owner would tell me to give the hard sell to gallery goers, I never felt confident to follow through and erred on the side of telling people to "go home and think about it." While honest and good advice, this did not help pay the bills. After a heartbreaking turn of events in which the family who owned the gallery lost a beloved member in 9/11, I found

myself unsure of everything in my life. I chose to leave my job and take a new one in an insurance brokerage firm.

YOU READ THAT RIGHT: INSURANCE BROKERAGE. SEXY STUFF.

At the time all I knew was that I wanted a steady paycheck while I figured things out. I had loved the people I'd met there during my interview and the camaraderie of a real, live office (complete with my own cubicle and free coffee—the American dream), so I took the job assuming it would be temporary as I looked for my true calling. One month turned into two and then I blinked and I had been there two years and promoted to an account manager role. What had I become? How did I end up spending mindless hours working on Excel spreadsheets and using vocabulary like "HIPAA laws" and "monthly premiums"?

But then it hit me—if I didn't make a change, I'd be there for another five years and totally, completely bored with my life. I found myself falling back in love with the things I grew up adoring: houses. I slowly started looking around for an entry level design job and found one with a Boston designer who had a modern aesthetic that was the opposite of what I had been exposed to my whole life. I marched into my manager's office and quit on the spot. I was scared to lose the security of my little cube and steady paycheck, but I knew it was the right decision.

As I worked for the designer that following year, I grew to appreciate a new palette and found myself accenting favorites from my traditional upbringing with modern flair. I felt so blessed to get sent on errands at the design center, where I could study and salivate over the gorgeous fabrics and furniture pieces. I started to feel that perhaps I had found what I was meant to do with my life. But then, out of the blue, I was let go right before my upcoming wedding. It was a vexing and upsetting turn of events, but one that broke me in the right places and made me ask myself some hard questions.

When I returned from my honeymoon, I found I was a bit soured by the design industry. I wasn't sure I was cut out for it and instead took a job planning alumnae events for an all-girls boarding school much like the one I had attended and loved. The cozy and familiar environment was nice, but I knew in my gut this job wasn't entirely right either. By this time, 2006, design blogs had started to get popular and after reading a few and toying with different blogging platforms, I figured I'd start my own simply as a way to catalog my ideas and feed my creative spirit while keeping my tidy little day job. At first only my mother and Andrew read it, but then I started seeing my site traffic tick up slowly. My friends were actually reading, and then some of their friends started too. I remember the day I went online and saw that seventy-five people had read the blog in one day and feeling like the most popular girl on earth. Perhaps there was something to this whole blogging thing.

I REMEMBER THE DAY I WENT ONLINE AND SAW THAT SEVENTY-FIVE PEOPLE HAD READ THE BLOG IN ONE DAY AND FEELING LIKE THE MOST POPULAR GIRL ON EARTH.

After about six months of posting every day for basically no one, I was asked by a friend of a friend to help with the decoration of their apartment. The budget was minuscule, but I could not have been more thrilled to have my first real client. As the blog took on more readers and a couple more people hired me for decorating help, it became clear that I had unknowingly started a business. Luckily I had married an incredibly supportive (and entrepreneurial) man who pushed me to take a chance, quit my job, and give myself a year to get my business off the ground. Not being a risk taker, this seemed completely INSANE to me, but after a lot of cautious debating and back and forth, I did it. I quit the last job I will ever have working for someone else.

Since then it's been a slow and steady build, one that has taken an immense amount of dedication. I've blogged every single weekday for the last seven years, over 2,700 posts. It baffles me to think I could possibly have that much to share, yet still, every morning when I wake up, I am so excited to post something for my readers. Beyond that, I have worked on so many amazing homes with many more to come and now get to employ other people—an amazing feat that fills me with honest-to-goodness joy every day. And yes, I even got to meet Oprah, which was like seeing a unicorn in the flesh, in case you were wondering.

People ask me how I did it, and I can tell you I am no more special or talented than the next blogger or designer out there. I simply show up every day, stay honest and open, and give my best to every person who flatters me by allowing me in to help decorate their home. I pride myself on never turning my nose up at a small project and always treating someone who is spending $2,000 with the same respect and dedication as one who's spending $200,000.

I have honest-to-goodness passion for what I do, and I think that makes all the difference in the world. I learned from seeing my dad go off to "work" on weekends and spend all his free time reading design magazines that when you love what you do, it never feels like work. And when you've found something that makes you feel that way, I would say you've found your calling.

OPPOSITE: Armoires make for wonderful storage units!

In my old studio,
chalkboard paint
made big blank
walls useful (and
pretty).

CREATING AN INSPIRING OFFICE

Not every home has a whole room to dedicate to office space, and not every person is in need of one either. Most people need an area to keep all paperwork, computers, and household bills. When I set up my first home office, I made sure it had two things: a door I could shut to keep me from being distracted during the day and thinking about work at night, and a decent amount of organizational space. Whether you are managing your household or a small business from your home office, you have to find a look and a system to make it inspirational and functional.

OPPOSITE: The smallest bedroom in our home serves as the office. I have always wanted a navy room, so I took the opportunity to try it out here (Benjamin Moore Blue Note), offsetting it with a wood desk in a light finish, modern chair, and linen-and-nailhead cornice. The brass-arrow sconces were a lucky vintage find!

DEFINE YOUR STYLE: OFFICE

modern

Lacquer desk, modernist chair, chrome, and pops of color.

eclectic

Inlay pattern desk, colored upholstery, silver, and Lucite.

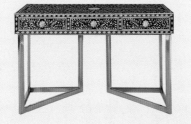

glamorous

Glass desk, bamboo chair, graphic tray, and whimsical touches.

traditional

Painted wood, slipcovered seating, old silver, and ginger jars.

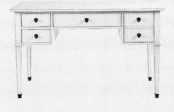

new country

Rustic wood, leather accents, wire mesh, and painted driftwood.

OPPOSITE: This small Beacon Hill office was painted high-gloss Hague Blue by Farrow & Ball and topped with a star wallpaper on the ceiling. Not stopping there, we added a print Roman shade, orange velvet chair, and zebra-hide rug to complete the bold, moody look.

LEFT: I found this chair, as is, at an antiques shop for under $100 and fell madly in love with it. The pillow is a funny little accent to keep the mood light, and the gilt-frame bulletin board holds inspirational images and notes.

USE A VARIETY OF FURNITURE

Don't limit yourself to just office chairs and desks. Look at small dining tables for desks and dining chairs for a comfortable place to sit. Dining room buffets and bedroom dressers also provide great storage in a home office without looking utilitarian. I've even found great office storage for adults at kids' furniture stores!

We updated this home office with grass-cloth wall coverings, patterned Roman shades, and a few upholstered items to soften it up.

BE REALISTIC ABOUT YOUR NEEDS

I've mentioned this tip before, but I will repeat myself because it's so important. A sleek desk and minimal places to conceal clutter and put away papers will leave you with a pretty but messy office. Outfit your room with a multitude of places to store away small items and organize your work. A clean office makes you more productive!

ABOVE, LEFT TO RIGHT: This dramatic Back Bay office space is part of a multipurpose room. The shagreen-wrapped desk with brass legs and custom-upholstered chair create a luxurious atmosphere against the dark wood paneling. • The modern lamp adds some unexpected attitude.

OPPOSITE: Two massive built-in bookshelves reside in this office, and the books within it complement the color scheme and décor of the room. Tip: visit vintage bookstores and buy old books in bulk from the bargain sections!

BE INSPIRED

You don't have to be in a creative or artistic career to create an inspiration board. Put a bulletin board on the wall in a place you can spot it from your desk and fill it with images that inspire your work. Maybe it's a vacation spot you hope to go to, or a car you want to get when you reach a career goal . . . anything that makes you feel driven and happy. Visual cues and reminders of what you are hoping to accomplish with all your hard work can really help motivate.

OPPOSITE, LEFT TO RIGHT: The wall of a guestroom holds this home's office space, made cheerful by the bright coral-orange and navy and a heavy dose of crisp white. Baskets serve as under-the-desk storage and a Michelle Armas print leans atop the desk. • The backs of this bookcase were painted deep chocolate so that accessories and books really pop.

We retrofitted and refinished this armoire as a secretary for a client in need of a small workspace within her open living room. If you don't have a room to dedicate as an office, a piece like this works fabulously!

CONCEAL THE DARN PRINTER

Ahhh, the printer. The elephant in the room in any home office. We can't avoid it, but we CAN conceal it. If you have an open-bottom desk, there are cabinets you can buy that conceal the printer and roll under the desk. Another idea is to skirt the desk in a great fabric and put the printer underneath it on a small shelf or box. When all else fails, buy a great console, small dresser, or bookshelf and accessorize around it!

TOP TIPS FOR BLOGGERS OLD AND NEW

1. SET A SCHEDULE: The best schedule is a new post every weekday, but if your schedule does not allow for that kind of time commitment, post on regularly scheduled days, like Monday, Wednesday, Friday, or once a week, but always on the same day. People like routine and don't want to waste time checking a blog that's updated haphazardly. They'll lose interest and move on.

2. HAVE A VOICE: People want to know more about you, and not just all the good and pretty things in your life. Share your struggles if you feel comfortable opening up, or discuss what's on your mind even if it's not on point. The more your readers know about you, the more loyal they will feel.

3. HIRE SOMEONE TO DEAL WITH THE TECHNICAL STUFF: I can barely change a font on my site myself. I learned to pay others who do that part of the business well and leave me to the curating and writing. You can find designers at all levels, from recent graphic design school graduates to seasoned vets in the industry. Nothing says "established" like a professionally designed blog. Side note: keep it simple and let the images and words stay center stage.

4. RESEARCH WHAT OTHERS ARE POSTING: There was a day when I happened to post about the same exact project as another design blogger without even knowing it. Someone accused me of copying them, when I had not even read their blog! It's good to keep up on other people's work, not only to stay informed and learn, but also to make sure your point of view is unique. (See number 2!)

OPPOSITE: We designed a fantastic kid's study area with funky ikat drapes, a modern light, and simple, contemporary furnishings.

5. GET IN ON THE DISCUSSION: As I said above, you need to read other blogs and get involved in the community of fellow bloggers. It's a great way to meet and interact with like-minded people and the best way to get new readership. When you strike up friendships and are nice, someone might post about you and get you some traffic! And once the ball starts rolling. . . .

6. ATTEND EVENTS: Get up from the computer and get your sassy self to some real events with REAL, live people! Have cards made up with your blog's name, web address, and your phone number and hand them out when you meet media people, others in your industry, and new friends. Word of mouth is the BEST marketing tool!

7. HAVE PATIENCE: Nothing happens overnight. You need to work at this every day and stay committed for the long haul in order for it to work. It can take a long time, but it's worth it!

8. IGNORE THE HATERS: Once you attain any kind of readership, you will have people leaving rude, thoughtless, and hurtful comments. Do your very best to ignore them, delete them if you wish, and move on. Conversing with them gives them the attention they crave and saps energy from your pursuits. I've made this mistake and learned from it!

9. MIX IT UP: Just because you are an interiors blogger or a foodie blogger does not mean you can never veer from your topic. I started doing just that—including fashion, pop culture, and deeply personal essays that greatly improved my readership. People like it when you mix it up!

10. MAKE SURE YOU ARE HAVING FUN: Readers can tell when your heart isn't in it—and it's a drag to spend so much time on something that isn't giving you joy. If you find your blog is more of a chore than an energy booster, think twice about what it is you are writing about, how you're writing, and why. Maybe you need to mix it up (as said above) or maybe you need a break. Listen to your instincts!

Custom-designed bookshelves
house a myriad of tomes.

THE CLOSET

FROM MULLETS TO MANOLOS

Knowing me now it may be hard for you to imagine, but as a little girl I wanted nothing to do with girly fashion. While my mom tried to get me into party dresses and bows, I just wanted to wear OshKosh B'gosh overalls and play with my brother outside building forts and riding bikes. I also apparently hated to shower and/or let my mom brush my hair, resulting in a VERY unfortunate mullet situation, which I rocked for most of the '80s. To say I was a tomboy is an understatement. A good example of my disdain for all things girly is reflected best in the time my mom took me to the mall to buy some patent leather dress shoes for Easter, and after she handed me the bag to carry like a "big girl," I promptly marched out into the mall,

OPPOSITE: While my closet isn't the grandest, to this former city dweller, it feels big. Adding luxe touches here and there makes it feel special no matter what the size—and don't forget to dress the windows, even those in the closets!

opened the box, and threw the shoes into a water fountain. There they floated, delighting me in their watery demise, while my mom probably considered putting me up for adoption. Soon thereafter my little brother got his head stuck between the metal bars surrounding the fountain and the fire department had to come pry him out. Needless to say, thanks to my dad being the mall's designer, that water fountain ceased to exist after the Tubridy kids had their way with it. Sorry for ruining the fun, everyone.

But growing up I spent a lot of time in that mall. Our family's clothing store, a small women's specialty store, had relocated there from its original location and I loved to "go to work" with my dad. In the family for three generations, that store was our family's legacy. My great-grandparents opened it after coming over from Ireland in 1916. After they passed away, my grandparents ran it, bringing my father up to be the next in line to hold the reins. In our town, it was an enduring institution, a place where the same ladies worked the floor for decades and knew your name and what size you wore. And when I saw strangers carrying bags emblazoned with the store logo (and my maiden name) I always brimmed with pride.

In fact, the store was the catalyst for my coming into being. It's how my parents met, my fetching mother a new salesgirl, and my dad the manager. Before long they had a few little rug rats playing hide-and-seek in the racks of Anne Klein, one of them being me. I like to think this is where it was all born, my love of pretty things. I loved roaming through the displays and seeing what new goodies my dad had bought on his buying trips to New York (a vast foreign land I pictured chock-full of racks and racks of pretty clothes—not far from reality, as it turns out). The back rooms contained what felt like a giant toy box of purses and earrings and scarves, headless mannequins, wigs, and rows and rows of empty hangers and shopping bags. I spent many a winter break back there with the in-house tailor, Maria, who supervised me in my first ever job wrapping packages at holiday time. It was such a delight, to get my corners perfect and pick the corresponding bows resulting in something wonderfully pretty for our customers. It was my introduction into the family business. Years later, I got to work

ABOVE: The family store circa the 1930s.

the floor as a salesgirl and I thought the store would always be a part of my life.

Sadly, it had to close in the '90s as the town's economy struggled and my dad's architectural design business took off. But even though that era was ending, I realized just how much I had learned about fashion from spending so many years among the dresses, sweaters, and "slacks" (as my grandfather called them). I absorbed so much about materials, colors, accessorizing, and how to put together outfits that it is no wonder that I eventually transformed from a tomboy into a fashion-obsessed preteen.

Around this time, I had my first fashion-related love affair. A pair of white leather cowgirl boots with fringe and silver studs. I'm not sure where I got them or how, all I remember is wearing them with EVERYTHING. Acid-washed pleated jeans? Wear the boots. Dress and tights? Wear the boots. Proper English-style horseback riding lessons? Skip the riding boots, wear the boots. While all the preppy little ladies saddled up on their horses in proper jodhpurs and black boots, I strutted out to my horse in bedazzled jeans, a puffy painted sweatshirt, and white fringed boots. I can just picture my always immaculately put-together mom shaking her head and laughing now.

It's only through experimenting and suffering some embarrassing missteps (for me, brocade vests, jelly shoes, hair crimpers, MC Hammer pants) that you learn to define your style. I'm still working on that myself, being a lover of many types of fashion, from tailored and preppy to bohemian and even edgy. But as holds true with interior design and other aesthetic pursuits, sometimes it's the mix of unrelated and opposite things that makes for the best outcome. As long as you love it, it looks good on you.

EDITING YOUR CLOSET

We've all been there—that moment you open your closet, glance at the full racks, shelves, and hooks and declare, "I hate everything and have nothing to wear." I had a moment like this recently and decided it was time for a serious edit. There were items hanging in my closet I had some strange affection for—a pink button-down shirt I hadn't worn in years, a skirt I bought my semester abroad in Manhattan (yes, that's absolutely "abroad" when you live in suburban Connecticut) that hadn't seen daylight since the last decade. Yet I still had these things for two reasons: 1. in case they came back in style and 2. in case of the .003 percent chance that one day I'd get dressed and really need them to complete an outfit. We all know these two reasons are total crap and complete excuses to hoard old stuff we don't need. Much like decorating, I am wonderful at helping others weed out clothes they should toss or donate.

But when it comes to my own wardrobe, I freeze in indecision. So I decided to treat myself like a client and took a ruthless, objective approach to editing and came up with these guidelines:

Set aside enough time to do this once and do it right. Don't give yourself an hour. Give yourself half a day or an entire day based on the size of your closet. If you try to cram it all into a short amount of time, you won't do a thorough or complete job. And, no, you won't "come back later" to finish. Do it once and do it well.

Start with a clean, full set of clothes. Pick up everything from the dry cleaner, do the wash, and then put the clothing away so that you are editing everything you own.

Have a plan. Start with your hanging clothes first, then move on to items in your dresser and on shelves, such as shoes, accessories, and undergarments. Or use whatever iteration of this process works for you. Compartmentalizing in this way allows you to feel less overwhelmed than you would if you dumped everything you own onto the bed.

The most important rules are those by which you consider whether a piece should be kept, donated, or tossed, and here they are:

KEEP IT if it's been worn in the last year more than once, is in good condition, is a classic-enough style to make it through two more seasons of wear, and fits you well—or could be tailored to fit you better and is worth the

investment and you'll actually go do it, not just say you'll do it!

DONATE IT OR CONSIGN IT if you have not worn it in the last year, it fits you poorly and is not worth getting tailored, you simply do not like it anymore, and/or it was truly a bad purchase. Just because it was expensive does not mean you HAVE to keep it. Cut your losses and move on to something you really love. This holds especially true for shoes that hurt your feet that you simply look at and never wear!

TOSS IT if it's in bad condition (holes, tears, stains) and is not appropriate for donation.

Sort the clothes into piles, including a "not sure" pile. Then invite a trusted friend who can be an honest judge over for coffee or a drink. Try everything on for them à la that montage in *Sex and the City*, the movie.

Box up the donations, consignments, and trash and get them out of the room. Now you have a clean slate and you can start organizing your closet, figuring out what you're missing. Make a list of things you need to fill out your wardrobe as you reorganize, e.g., "new black pencil skirt" or "more day-to-night dresses." Keep this list with you in your wallet as a reminder for when you are out shopping.

Do your best to keep your space like this until the next time you need to do an edit, but know that we ALL end up with messy closets sometimes, so give yourself a break.

I think you'll find that once you just get rid of the clutter of ugly, old, and unloved things in your closet you'll find it easier to get dressed and easier to shop smart.

OPPOSITE: One of the house's original details I kept were the glass and brass doorknobs.

ABOVE, LEFT TO RIGHT: I love keeping delicate necklaces organized by draping them on this vintage hand sculpture. • Metallic wallpaper and a new feminine light add some glamour.

STRIPED LONG SLEEVE TEE

CLASSIC BLACK HEELS

CASHMERE TURTLENECK

WELL-MADE LEATHER BAG

A PREPPY TUNIC

INVEST IN THE BEST

So, where exactly should you spend your hard-earned money and where should you save? You've probably heard that basics, not trends, are where you should invest—but what is considered a basic? Basics are not the same to all women—one may wear more blazers and heels, while another may wear jeans and flats most days. Here are my picks for great basics that will get you through just about any occasion. Spend once smartly instead of twice stupidly!

AN ICONIC TRENCH

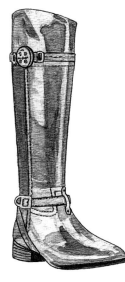

LEATHER RIDING BOOTS

BLACK OR NAVY BLAZER

JEANS THAT FLATTER
(ANY CUT THAT WORKS FOR YOU)

PERFECT-FITTING BLACK DRESS

AN HEIRLOOM WATCH

LEOPARD FLATS
(A NEUTRAL, I SWEAR!)

OPPOSITE: What girl wouldn't want this walk-in closet? We papered the ceiling with a silver chevron pattern and added a clear glass chandelier.

LEFT: A Lucite console offers up a place to keep jewelry where the owner can see it—and a spot to prop up tall boots too!

CLOSET TO COUCH

If you feel unsure about what kind of colors you should use in your home, look to your closet for hints. Typically you will notice a theme, such as tailored and neutral basics, bold and patterned colors, or lots of greens and blues. What looks best on your body will also delight you on your sofa.

GET IT ORGANIZED

There are so many great options for closet systems these days, from Ikea to custom. Figure out exactly the kind of storage you need and design a system around that. Use every possible inch to your advantage. Baskets, bins, and small dressers help you keep jewelry, shoes, small bags, and the dreaded sweater avalanche controlled and contained. The simple addition of small wall hooks behind your hanging clothes is wonderful for keeping scarves and belts off the floor!

DRESS IT UP

Closets are functional spaces, but that doesn't mean they can't also be pretty. Add some decorative touches to your closet to make it a place you want to keep neat and tidy (and spend time in!). I love to accessorize and decorate closets—my favorite trick is to install wallpaper on the ceiling! You get a big bang for your buck, since usually you don't need a large amount of paper. Swap your basic ceiling light with something fancier and invest in matching velvet-coated hangers. You'll be surprised at the difference a small change like that makes!

renter's tip

Rental apartment closets aren't typically fitted out with fancy closet systems. But don't fret. You can create your own closet system with a carefully organized mix of freestanding shelving, stackable plastic bins with drawers, fabric-covered boxes, and baskets found at most big home-improvement chain stores.

ABOVE: The closet island serves as jewelry and accessory storage.

OPPOSITE: The most stylish little girl gets to call this closet hers, with the interior papers in a violet bouclé print and lots of built-ins for organization.

OPPOSITE: In this grand Chicago walk-in closet we added some attitude with a graphic wallpaper on the ceiling and behind all the shelving, as well as leopard window seats and trimmed shades.

ABOVE: Treat your closet shelves like boutique displays to make getting ready a fun experience.

THE SUNROOM
& OUTDOOR
SPACES

DIGGING UP THE DIRT

I find nothing more relaxing than wrapping up a busy day with a glass of wine on a sunny patio. I spend as much time as I can outdoors in warmer months, so when we moved into our new house, we were determined to craft the patio of our dreams in the lumpy, overgrown backyard by the summer of our first year there. We finally got our act together, drew up some plans, and hired a crew to start making things happen. What can go wrong when you're just putting in a small paver patio, you ask? Oh, only really bad, weird stuff, that's all.

A little backstory: the original owner of our house happened to be an embalmer. Not only did our Realtor tell us this, but our construction crew found some old embalming fluid in our basement

OPPOSITE: We adore spending time outside and our patio was designed to allow us to entertain and relax comfortably. Modern Ikea chairs surround a vintage-looking drum table while the fire pit roars beside.

before

when we were renovating the kitchen. Not creepy at all. A work-from-home embalmer, is that even a thing? So from day one I've been a little preoccupied with this fact. Before we even closed on the house, I almost had part of the yard excavated for dead bodies due to a specific little garden plot that was the exact shape and size of a casket. Coincidence? I thought not. Thank goodness I was wrong.

Talked down from my "graveyard" obsession, we never really gave the whole thing another thought. But when the guys arrived to excavate the backyard for the patio, I jokingly said to them over my morning coffee as they started digging, "Hey, the guy who built this house was an embalmer, so if you hit any caskets or corpses, let me know." Everyone got a good chuckle out of that one. Ha, ha, ha.

But then a couple of hours later my phone rang. It was my friend, who was overseeing the project for me, and she said with a worried tone, "Um, so, the guys hit something in the backyard."

"You mean like a big rock?" I asked.

"No, more like a big rectangle box. . . ."

"UHHHHH, A COFFIN? THEY HIT A COFFIN?"

"We don't know yet; they're still digging it out. I'll call you back."

I knew it! Dead bodies in the yard! Justified at last! (And totally grossed out too.)

ABOVE: Our boring backyard before we began, and the startling surprise we found during excavation. It is still a mystery!

Andrew went home and started sending me pictures of what these guys were uncovering. And it was some scary stuff, as you can see here. Once they were done, they uncovered a 9 x 3-foot iron box filled with dirt right smack in the middle of my backyard. No one had any clue what it was. Clearly, since it was metal it wasn't a coffin (except maybe one for zombies), but it also wasn't a septic tank, a root cellar, or any of the other things we could think of. None of the workers had ever seen anything like it. Seeing as our soil was so incredibly fertile, I fancied it a tank where he kept all the drained blood from the dead bodies. No one else seemed to think that was possible and looked at me like I was a psychopath dressed in J.Crew. Regardless, it took three men two full days to cut that thing apart with metal saws and get it out of the ground. Oh, and a nice big bill of $2,600 to do so. Stupid mystery coffin. *So much for new fall clothes,* I thought.

Our neighbors claimed it had been a fish pond at one point, but I still like to think it was something far more sinister; it makes for a better story. Of course, now it's gone and in its place is a gorgeous patio where we spend countless hours of enjoyment. For me, it's another example of how we have to go through dark times and unearth some pretty yucky stuff

WITHOUT OUR TRIALS AND TRIBULATIONS, THE SWEET DOESN'T TASTE QUITE AS DELECTABLE, NOW, DOES IT?

in order to come out on the other side with something beautiful. This entire house, from the beginning, was something I didn't think I could stomach. The shabby exterior, dated and dusty interior, and a myriad of problems we uncovered in the process of making it a home we now love has actually turned out to be the reason we now are so happy here. Not unlike life itself. Without our trials and tribulations, the sweet doesn't taste quite as delectable, now, does it?

This little life lesson isn't new for me, and most likely not for you either. Some of my most painful times have resulted in the best outcomes that have made my life so much better. After my bout of anorexia and yearlong stint in a mental hospital fighting to get better, I felt I couldn't go back to my high school. I hated the idea of being thought of as the girl who went away to the loony bin and knew my uneducated peers were whispering about me having cancer and even AIDS. Still fragile and not completely well, my parents bravely let me apply to Miss Porter's School, an all-girls boarding school famed for its fancy alumnae and proper reputation. Upon visiting, I found it to be the exact opposite of its snobby reputation, full of warm, interesting, and smart women. I was accepted and managed to stay well enough to start anew the following year.

No one knew what I had been through, and so no one judged me for it. I was welcomed with open arms into a loving community of people who wanted to see me thrive. And thrive I did—not only coming out of my shy, self-conscious shell but being elected captain of the JV field hockey team within two months on campus, and then the following year establishing a new cross-country team, traveling to Italy for the first time, and, finally, being elected to one of the eight coveted heads of school positions in a schoolwide election. This broken girl, once slowly killing herself, had been saved.

Attending that school is what changed my life. I can't fathom who I'd be today had I not gone there. And the only way I could have and did get there was by going through something horrible. So when you find yourself going through a dark time, embrace it and try to learn from it. Push up your sleeves, take on a challenge, and get into the thick of things. Try something new and scary, bite off more than you can chew . . . buy a house you have to work on and toil with to make right. Sometimes it simply will not work out. And in those times, you will learn more than when you get it right. After all, in the end, it's the journey that defines us, not the destination.

RIGHT: Who doesn't like a good backyard cocktail hour?

OPPOSITE: We hope to rebuild this room soon, but in the meantime it has turned out to be the space we use the most in warmer months. An indoor/outdoor Dash and Albert rug covers the ugly linoleum floor and a discount site sofa is pepped up with some foliage-print pillows. And, of course, we have to have a dog bed for the "kids."

LEFT: Lucky scores from a couple of bargain shops helped me create this little moment in front of the room's brick wall. A raw-edged console and gilded peacock mirror really amp up the glamour while a leather butterfly chair provides a comfy place to sit. I found the concrete elephant at a flea market!

DESIGNING A CHEERY SUNROOM

Don't limit yourself to outdoor furniture in this space. Combine standard interior pieces with a few more outdoor-style items to make this space effective as a transition from indoors to outdoors. Sturdy fabric choices that resist fading (such as outdoor fabrics) and indoor-outdoor rugs that can be easily cleaned will allow you to relax and enjoy this open-air room. I treat my sunroom as an extension of the living room in the summer, so I made sure the color scheme and furniture styles casually related to the rest of the interior furniture. A pop of color is a good idea in this type of room as it creates an uplifting mood.

CLOCKWISE FROM TOP LEFT: A brass bar cart sits below images taken by the homeowners on a safari honeymoon. • The massive Buddha gets a lift from a custom-made bronze base. • This ikat-stripe upholstery mixed with a floral pillow in coordinating colors feels just perfect.

OPPOSITE: We gave this architecturally gorgeous sunroom new life with pops of deep violet and rich orange. A mix of modern and traditional furniture creates a playful yet mature look while the client's massive wood Buddha oversees the scene.

BRING THE GREEN IN

One of the best ways to inject color and life into any room is to add plants. A living thing, be it a bouquet of flowers or a tree, adds so much depth and texture. I love using fiddle leaf fig trees in empty corners of living rooms. Their sculptural quality adds so much to a space and may be just the thing you're missing! Keeping them alive is a whole other ballgame, though. Placing an orchid or even a simple bouquet of grocery-store-bought blooms on a table does wonders for your home and your mood.

OPPOSITE: Bringing the outside in by adding greenery, plants, and flowers to your interior decoration is such an important detail! Nothing brings life to a room like a touch of green. If you don't have a green thumb, consider succulents, easy-to-tend-to plants and trees, or long-lasting orchids.

PRETTYING UP THE PATIO

Long gone are the days of mesh and metal chairs and cheesy-print outdoor cushions. Today there are a myriad of great-looking outdoor furniture options to use in any outdoor space, from a small city deck to a palatial country patio.

—Not everything has to match! A lot of patio furniture is sold in sets, but don't feel like you have to buy every single piece. When able, mix in a couple of styles of furniture to avoid looking too matchy-matchy.

—Patterned outdoor throw pillows make a HUGE difference in livening up a plain furniture set. Check Etsy (www.etsy.com) for pillow covers made from designer outdoor fabrics, and be sure the inserts are all-weather to avoid mold!

OPPOSITE, CLOCKWISE FROM TOP LEFT: This raised bed was made out of additional paver stones to give us a great place to plant tall grasses to conceal an otherwise ugly fence. • The depth and width of the porch and steps were designed to be additional seating when need be. • My grandparents' vintage Brown Jordan dining set was powder-coated glossy black and topped with striped outdoor cushions for the perfect spot to eat a meal off the grill.

ABOVE: In the heart of the city is this great patio, complete with outdoor kitchen and comfortable woven seating for a host of people. Bright blue-and-green accents reflect the color scheme of the interior through the glass doors.

—Lighting is just as important outside as it is inside. From string lights to solar lanterns and hardwired outdoor sconces, be sure to add lighting on different levels (and so people can see what they're eating when dining al fresco!).

—When choosing material for your outdoor space, be conscious of the climate. If you live in an area where there are deep freezes, avoid stamped or solid concrete slab as it can crack. Stone is expensive but the most natural looking, while more affordable options are brick or concrete pavers (which these days mimic stone quite closely).

ABOVE: Dinner is set for two at this faux bamboo dining table (with the gold Massachusetts State House dome in the distance).

OPPOSITE: We wanted to give this roof deck some furniture as nice as its views. A corner sectional, a modern coffee table, and yellow accents all make for a happy place to lounge.

GREEN AND GLORIOUS GARDENS

My mother's garden is incredible—you get a taste of it here from these photos, but in person it's really something to behold. After having to jump headlong into gardening with my few simple beds, I now appreciate more than ever the incredibly hard work that goes into creating and maintaining green spaces like hers. Of course, she was a huge help in getting my yard to look as lovely as it does, so I wanted to share her helpful tips with you too!

TOP GARDENING TIPS FROM MOM

—Trial and error is a forgivable gardener's sin! Experiment with color, shapes, plant varieties, and interesting textures. There are so few opportunities in life where one can be creative and nurturing, and where mistakes just aren't a big deal.

—Perennials give you great positive feedback when, after the worst of winters, they emerge again in the spring! In choosing new plants, shop early at the garden centers and pick the healthiest-looking specimens. It is important to read the tags on plants, as they provide all the information that you need to keep the plants you've chosen happy. Will the flowers fit in with your color scheme? How tall and wide will they grow? Do they require full sun or full shade?

OPPOSITE, CLOCKWISE FROM TOP LEFT: Pots and birdhouses decorate the property. • A simple detail, like this star cutout in the garden gate, adds personality. • My parents' charming back garden and patio, tended by my mother.

—Generally speaking, a perennial garden should be arranged with smaller plants in the front and the taller specimens toward the back of the plot. Try to include boulders, other garden objects, and lots of pots brimming with annuals. Birdhouses and birdbaths also add visual interest to a garden.

—Take time to prepare your garden soil. Add compost or manure annually to even out your existing beds. Not only does it give them the extra boost they need, it also loosens the soil. For new beds you can use packaged garden soil from the store. Your garden will pay you back in spades for the effort put in at the beginning of the season!

—Place your new plants in the garden while still in their pots so that you can eyeball the design. Do one section at a time and only buy plants that you can put in the ground that day. If your eyes are bigger than the hours you have, some of the plants will dry out and die in their pots before you get back to planting them.

—All good things come to an end, however. During the season, dead flower heads should be removed to encourage more flowers to take their places. At the end of the growing season, everything must be cut down according to the recommendations on the plant label which you read and hopefully even saved!

—Miracle-Gro is true to its name—USE OFTEN.

ABOVE, LEFT TO RIGHT: It's exhausting to picture my mother planting six hundred little plants between the flagstones on her patio, but over time they grew in and really make for a gorgeous and natural groundcover. • A pretty robin's-egg-blue gourd birdhouse nestled into the clematis.

OPPOSITE: The bluestone front patio at my parents' house overlooks a gorgeous green field.

OPPOSITE: The back of our house was flat, with no real access to the backyard. We added this glass door, decking, and trellises to define and enhance the exterior. Thanks to my green-thumbed mom, we have lots of pretty potted gardens to dress it up with as well.

LEFT: Another small container garden nestled into the real garden!

POTS, CONTAINER GARDENS, AND WINDOW BOXES

Pots and planter boxes can make a big impact for relatively little work and maintenance. They can be moved around to provide interest where you need it. If you have no room for a garden plot, a gorgeous collection of interesting pots and window boxes can satisfy the gardening urges of even the most devoted gardeners.

—Choose pots that are not too heavy. Many pots are made of composites that hold the moisture better and won't crack, and they truly look very real! It is hard to beat the classic gorgeousness of an aged, mossy, clay pot. Plants in clay pots need to be watered much more frequently than those in plastic or composite pots.

—Use either pea stones, broken pot shards, or packing peanuts in the bottom of the container. Upon that, layer potting soil. Many good potting soils have plant food in them, and some have pellets that retain moisture. Leave room at the top of the pots for your plants, of course.

—A basic container includes a larger, unique plant in the center with several smaller plants around it, filled in by some type of draping plant. You can combine annuals and perennials, changing out the annuals as the season changes.

—Moss is your friend when planting pots and planters. After the plants are firmly and tightly snuggled in, the moss goes on top between the stems. In the case of window boxes, it helps keep dirt from scattering up onto the house. In pots, it not only looks pretty, but the moss helps retain moisture too!

CLOCKWISE FROM TOP LEFT: Varying the heights of plants really helps fill out embankments and beds. • Small or large, adding planter gardens to your patio makes for charming little moments. • Our little house, small on size but big on style. • Our little shed (or "the barn" as we call it) was painted a deep green-gray and dressed up with a new window box. • Window boxes on the front of my parents' home.

ACKNOWLEDGMENTS

No book is ever a solo endeavor, so I have plenty of people to thank in helping me achieve this incredible dream. To my agent, Kathryn Beaumont Murphy, for believing in this idea and making it come to life, and Trish Todd and everyone at Simon & Schuster for trusting me and helping me to craft something worthy.

Thanks to my dedicated and incredible assistants—Lindsey Retelle, for keeping the ship afloat and being my right hand through it all, and Allison Whittemore, who kept all the details straight with her ninjalike organizational skills (of which I have none).

To Michael Lee, Michael Partenio, Sarah Winchester, Danielle Moss, and Eric Roth for their incredible images and ability to help me enjoy the process of shooting the images for this book.

To Stacy Kunstel for her wonderful eye and magical personality, and Jen Garran for her awesome, confidence-boosting pep talks and advice.

A big thank-you to my AMAZING clients whose homes they trusted me to decorate and shoot for this book: Natalie and Jeff Schwartz, Debra Brodsky and Erich Shigley, Dina Ciarimboli, Kirstan Barnett, Kelly O'Donnell, Lucas and Caitlin Turton, Jaimee Healy, Eileen Roscoe, Elizabeth Sheehan, Catherine Choquette and Lauren Zirilli. A big high five to Manny Makkas for whipping together pillows, drapes, and pelmets with twenty-four hours' notice without complaint.

A special thanks to my brothers for giving me some of my funniest material, my parents for being the best source of confidence, advice, and love a child could ever have, and, of course, my husband, Andrew. Without him I never would have been able to do any of this. He is the best cheerleader anyone could have in this life and his unwavering support makes me feel like the luckiest girl in the world. Oh, and he's funny, smart, and devastatingly handsome too (I told him I'd put that in print).

But most of all, the most heartfelt thank-you goes to my blog readers, old and new. Your dedication and support have allowed me to live my dreams and create a life I could never have imagined for myself. I consider you all my friends and I am eternally grateful for you every single day.

This small condo's galley kitchen was demolished to make way for a modern, open space. I worked with designer Justine Sterling on this project, and the results are incredible.

DESIGN RESOURCE GUIDE

My favorite spots to shop for clients (and myself!)
* Indicates a to-the-trade-only resource.

FURNITURE

ABC Carpet & Home
www.abchome.com

Arteriors Home
www.arteriorshome.com

Ballard Designs
www.ballarddesigns.com

Bernhardt*
www.bernhardt.com

Bradshaw Kirchofer
www.bradshawkirchofer.com

Bungalow 5*
www.bungalow5.com

Cisco Brothers
www.ciscobrothers.com

Crate&Barrel
www.crateandbarrel.com

Design Within Reach
www.dwr.com

Duralee*
www.duralee.com

Emerson et Cie*
www.emersonetcie.com

Furbish Studio
www.furbishstudio.com

Huston & Company
www.hustonandcompany.com

Jayson Home
www.jaysonhome.com

Jonathan Adler
www.jonathanadler.com

Lee Industries*
www.leeindustries.com

Lillian August*
www.lillianaugust.com

Plexi-Craft
www.plexi-craft.com

Pottery Barn
www.potterybarn.com

Knoll
www.knoll.com

Mitchell Gold + Bob Williams
www.mgbwhome.com

The New Traditionalists
www.thenewtraditionalists.com

Redford House*
www.redfordhouse.com

Restoration Hardware
www.restorationhardware.com

Room & Board
www.roomandboard.com

Society Social
www.shopsocietysocial.com

West Elm
www.westelm.com

Wisteria
www.wisteria.com

Williams-Sonoma
Williams-Sonoma Home
www.williams-sonoma.com

Worlds Away*
www.worlds-away.com

HOME ACCESSORIES

ABC Carpet & Home
www.abchome.com

Aerin
www.aerin.com

Anthropologie
www.anthropologie.com

Arteriors Home
www.arteriorshome.com

Ballard Designs
www.ballarddesigns.com

Biscuit Home
www.biscuit-home.com

Bungalow 5*
www.bungalow5.com

Calypso St. Barth
www.calypsostbarth.com

Canvas
www.canvashomestore.com

Crate & Barrel
www.crateandbarrel.com

Dwell Studio
www.dwellstudio.com

Furbish Studio
www.furbishstudio.com

Horchow
www.horchow.com

Hudson
www.hudsonboston.com

Jill Rosenwald
www.jillrosenwald.com

Jonathan Adler
www.jonathanadler.com

Kelly Wearstler
www.kellywearstler.com

Lawrence McRae Ceramics
www.lawrencemcrae.com

Liz Caan Interiors
www.lizcaaninteriors.com

Lekker
www.lekkerhome.com

Lulu & Georgia
www.luluandgeorgia.com

Plantation
www.plantationdesign.com

Pottery Barn
www.potterybarn.com

Restoration Hardware
www.restorationhardware.com

Shoppe by Amber Interiors
www.amberinteriordesign.
myshopify.com

Studio 534*
www.s5boston.com

Terrain
www.shopterrain.com

West Elm
www.westelm.com

Williams-Sonoma
Williams-Sonoma Home
www.williams-sonoma.com

Wisteria
www.wisteria.com

Zinc Door
www.zincdoor.com

Z Gallerie
www.zgallerie.com

ARTWORK

Michelle Armas, Fine Artist
www.michellearmas.com

Doug Foltz, Fine Artist
www.dougfoltz.com

Mallory Page, Fine Artist
www.mallorypage.com

Robert Rea Paintings, Fine
Artist
www.robertreapaintings.com

Kerri Rosenthal Art, Fine
Artist
www.kerrirosenthalart.com

Amanda Stone Talley,
Fine Artist
www.amandatalley.com

Etsy
www.etsy.com

The Iris Gallery of Fine Art
www.irisgallery.net

Jules Place
www.julesplace.com

Natural Curiosities
www.naturalcuriosities.com

Saatchi Online
www.saatchionline.com

Soicher Marin
www.soicher-marin.com

Society6
www.society6.com

Antiques and Vintage Goods:
1stdibs
www.1stdibs.com

Circa Who
www.circawho.com

eBay
www.ebay.com

Palm Beach Regency
www.palmbeachregency.com

Ruby Lane
www.rubylane.com

PAINT

Behr
www.behr.com

Benjamin Moore
www.benjaminmoore.com

Clark + Kensington
www.acehardware.com

Farrow & Ball
www.farrow-ball.com

Pratt & Lambert
www.prattandlambert.com

Sherwin-Williams
www.sherwin-williams.com

Valspar
www.valsparpaint.com

RUGS & FLOORING

ABC Carpet & Home
www.abchome.com

Calypso St. Barth
www.calypsostbarth.com

Dash & Albert Rug Company
www.dashandalbert.com

Flor
www.flor.com

Jill Rosenwald
www.jillrosenwald.com

Landry & Arcari
www.landryandarcari.com

Lulu & Georgia
www.luluandgeorgia.com

Madeline Weinrib
www.madelineweinrib.com

Merida*
www.meridameridian.com

Mohr & McPherson
www.mohr-mcpherson.com

Restoration Hardware
www.restorationhardware.com

RugsUSA.com
www.rugsusa.com

Stark*
www.starkcarpet.com

West Elm
www.westelm.com

LIGHTING

Arteriors Home
www.arteriorshome.com

Barbara Cosgrove Lamps*
www.barbaracosgrovelamps
.com

Hudson Valley Lighting
www.hudsonvalleylighting
.com

Lamps Plus
www.lampsplus.com

Schoolhouse Electric &
Supply Company
www.schoolhouseelectric.com

Shades of Light
www.shadesoflight.com

Rejuvenation
www.rejuvenation.com

Restoration Hardware
www.restorationhardware.com

Robert Abbey, Inc.*
www.robertabbey.biz

The Urban Electric Co.*
www.urbanelectricco.com

Visual Comfort*
Circa Lighting
www.visualcomfort.com
www.circalighting.com

TEXTILES &
WALLCOVERINGS

Cowtan & Tout*
www.cowtan.com

Duralee*
www.duralee.com

Jasper*
Michael S. Smith
www.michaelsmithinc.com

Katie Ridder*
www.katieridder.com

Kravet*
www.kravet.com

Lee Jofa*
www.leejofa.com

Lewis & Sheron Textiles
www.lsfabrics.com

Mally Skok Design*
www.mallyskokdesign.com

Osborne & Little*
www.osborneandlittle.com

Peter Dunham Textiles*
www.peterdunham.com

Phillip Jeffries*
www.phillipjeffries.com

Premier Prints
www.premierprintsinc.com

Samuel & Sons
Passementerie*
www.samuelandsons.com

Schumacher*
www.fschumacher.com

Spoonflower
www.spoonflower.com

Quadrille Fabrics*
www.quadrillefabrics.com

Zoffany*
www.zoffany.com

SHOWROOMS

DO Group*
www.fdogroup.com

Furn & Co*
www.furnco.us

Studio 534*
www.s5boston.com

Webster & Company*
www.webstercompany.com

BED & BATH

Biscuit Home
www.biscuit-home.com

Crane & Canopy
www.craneandcanopy.com

Dwell Studio
www.dwellstudio.com

John Robshaw Textiles
www.johnrobshaw.com

Matouk
www.matouk.com

Leontine Linens
www.leontinelinens.com

Pendleton Woolen Mills
www.pendleton-usa.com

Pottery Barn
www.potterybarn.com

Restoration Hardware
www.restorationhardware.com

Serena & Lily
www.serenaandlily.com

West Elm
www.westelm.com

Williams-Sonoma
Williams-Sonoma Home
www.williams-sonoma.com

OFFICE & PAPER GOODS

dabney lee
www.dabneylee.com

iomoi
www.iomoi.com

Poppin
www.poppin.com

See Jane Work
www.seejanework.com

KITCHEN & BATH

Ann Sacks
www.annsacks.com

Restoration Hardware
www.restorationhardware.com

Tile Showcase
www.tileshowcase.com

WaterSpot Showrooms
www.water-spot.com

Waterworks
www.waterworks.com

Williams-Sonoma
www.williams-sonoma.com

CHILDREN

ducduc
www.ducducnyc.com

Dwell Studio
www.dwellstudio.com

fawn&forest
www.fawnandforest.com

giggle
www.giggle.com

The Land of Nod
www.landofnod.com

Nursery Works
www.nurseryworks.net

Oeuf
www.oeufnyc.com

Pottery Barn Kids
www.potterybarnkids.com

Serena & Lily
www.serenaandlily.com

RH Baby & Child
www.rhbabyandchild.com

Rikshaw Design
www.rikshawdesign.com

WINDOWS

Ballard Designs
www.ballarddesigns.com

Pottery Barn
www.potterybarn.com

Restoration Hardware
www.restorationhardware.com

Serena & Lily
www.serenaandlily.com

Smith + Noble
www.smithandnoble.com

The Shade Store
www.theshadestore.com

West Elm
www.westelm.com

ILLUSTRATION CREDITS

PHOTOGRAPHY CREDITS

Gates, Erin—pages 23 (far right), 57 (far right), 75, 216, 276, 281, 299 (except bottom right)

Lee, Michael J.—cover, pages v, vi, viii, 10, 13, 17–20, 24, 26–28, 30–31, 52–59, 61, 62, 64–68, 76–79, 82, 87 (far left), 92–94, 98–99, 102, 105, 108 (top), 109, 112, 115, 122 (left), 123–127, 129–131, 134–135, 138–139, 157–158, 160–162, 163, 184–185, 188–190, 191, 192–193, 195–197, 199, 210–215, 218–219, 221, 232–233, 236–241, 243 (bottom left), 258, 260–266, 269, 301–303, 314

Litchfield, Sean—page 230

Moss, Danielle—pages xii, 29, 284–285

Partenio, Michael—pages ii, 2, 8, 11, 12, 22, 23 (except far right), 36, 39, 44–48 (top two), 49–51, 60, 87 (right two), 91, 106, 122 (right), 132, 136–137, 144, 148–149, 150–155, 156, 159, 163, 170, 174–175, 177–178, 182–183, 186–187, 194, 202, 205, 207–208, 217, 218, 220, 224, 227, 243 (except bottom left), 254, 259, 272, 277, 280, 282–283, 288, 292–293, 294–297, 300, 308, 311, 319

Partenio, Michael, for *Better Homes & Gardens*—pages xi, 25, 70–73, 191, 246, 251–253

Roth, Eric—pages 74, 138, 299 (bottom right)

Winchester, Sarah—pages 16, 48 (bottom), 63, 69, 108 (bottom), 128, 147, 234–235, 290, 304–306, 309, 310, 312, 320 (headshot)

The counters, pages 96–97:
Granite: Luis Carlos Torres/Shutterstock.com
Concrete: ©iStock.com/t_kimura
Marble: Jodie Johnson/Shutterstock.com
Quartz: StevanZZ/Shutterstock.com
Butcher Block: hawkeye978/Shutterstock.com
Soapstone: Stocksnapper/Shutterstock.com

ILLUSTRATION CREDITS

Harwell McElhaney, Anne—pages 32–33, 100–101, 164–167, 198, 278–279

SPECIAL IMAGE CREDITS

How to Hang Art, pages 164–167:
The Gallery Wall: Jenny Komenda Interiors/Nicole Franzen Photography
The Leaner: Carol LeFlufy/Marcia Prentiss Photography
The Bookworm: Ethan Feirstein & Ari Heckman via Lonny
The Statement: James Leland Day/Mike Newling Photography
The Grid: Eileen Kathryn Boyd via Traditional Home
The Balance: Phoebe Howard/Erika Dines Photography
The Vertical: Lisa and Mark Poulier via Homelife Australia
The Fine Mix: Anya Kucheryavenko

CHAPTER OPENER IMAGES

The Entry: Schumacher, Mughal Leaf

The Living Room: Schumacher, The Martyn Lawrence Bullard | Wallcoverings Collection, Darya Ikat Sidewall

The Kitchen: Schumacher, The Alessandra Branca Collection, Branca Stripe

The Dining Room: Schumacher, The Chroma Collection, Betwixt

The Family Room: Schumacher, The Natural Accents | Wallcoverings Featuring Celerie Kemble Collection, Ripple

The Bedroom, back cover: Schumacher, The Designer Favorites Collection, Pyne Hollyhock Print

The Bathroom: Brunschwig & Fils, The Hommage Collection, Yuzen Black

The Nursery: Schumacher, The Avant Garde | Wallcoverings Collection, Moonpennies

The Office: Brunschwig & Fils, Staccato Linen and Cotton Print

The Closet: Schumacher, The Modern Nature | Wallcoverings Collection, Shantung Silhouette Print

The Sunroom & Outdoor Spaces: Schumacher, The Chroma Collection, Vientiane Ikat Print

Endpapers: Duralee, Kipling Animal Prints & Wovens Collection

ERIN GATES is a Boston-based interior designer, blogger, and curator of all things stylish. Having spent years trying to find the perfect job to fulfill all her creative desires relating to art, design, fashion, and writing, she began her blog, *Elements of Style*, in 2007 and formed her own design company, Erin Gates Design, shortly thereafter. Soon she was designing homes from Boston to New York to Washington, DC, and even a sailboat in San Francisco. Her approach to design is a mix of new and old, high- and low-end, and modern and traditional. Erin's design work and writing is infused with her fresh, open, honest take on life, which has garnered thousands of readers the world over. Her designs and writing have been featured in publications such as *O, the Oprah Magazine, Ladies' Home Journal, House Beautiful, Boston Magazine, Inside Weddings,* and *Better Homes and Gardens*. Born in Connecticut, she is a graduate of Miss Porter's School and Connecticut College. She is married to Andrew Gates and is mom to her two furry kids, Baxter and Oliver.

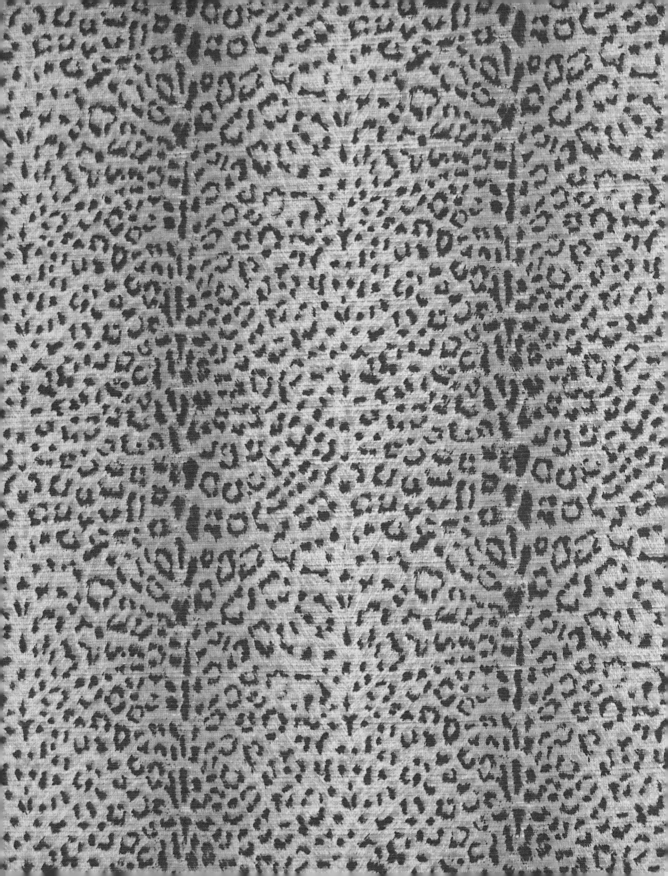